AF425280

When Silence Isn't Golden

Why the silent treatment damages relationships and how to repair the bridge back to healthy communication

Carol Stockdale

Copyright © 2022 Carol Stockdale

All rights reserved. No part of this book may be reproduced or transmitted in any form or by any means, electronic or mechanical, including photocopying, recording or by any information storage and retrieval system without permission in writing from the publisher.

EMCAR PRESS— Stroudsburg, PA
ISBN: 979-8-9872053-0-3
eBook 979-8-9872053-1-0
Library of Congress Control Number: 2022921868
Title: *Silence Isn't Golden: Why the silent treatment damages relationships and how to repair the bridge back to healthy communication*
Author: Carol Stockdale
Digital distribution | 2022
Paperback | 2022

Stockdalec31@gmail.com

Disclaimer

This author is not engaged in rendering psychological or medical services and this book is not intended as a guide to diagnose or treat psychological or medical problems.

Dedication

To my mother and to all who have been affected by silence

Bridge the Gap with words

Simple – Truthful - Genuine

© 2016 Frank Sonnenberg. All rights reserved.

Acknowledgments

I would like to thank and acknowledge with love and gratitude my children, Carolyn and Todd who engage me in all areas of conversation.

To my five grandchildren:

Ryan - who isn't afraid to share his emotions and thoughts.

Alex – whose story he wrote about me inspired me to write this book.

Carter – whose ability to adapt to change encouraged me to keep moving forward in my writing.

Mary – for her balance, organization, faith and wisdom

Emily – for her enthusiasm, compassion and laughter

To Diane Pallitto a special thank you for walking this journey with me. She was a great book coach and an excellent collaborator in the writing of this book and keeping me focused. Her faithful dedication and encouragement of the importance of the subject matter never waivered. I could not have accomplished this without her.

To Reuben Simpson who has taught me tolerance and how communication can unite us. A big thank you for the gift of a new computer for this venture.

Thank you to Melinda Cross who kept my voice while editing my random thoughts and her constant enthusiastic support.

Thank you, Rev. Sherry Blackman for feeling my passion for the subject matter. Your willingness to take time from your busy schedule to give me guidance, support and direction was much appreciated.

Thank you Em Hughes, Executive Publisher of New Book Authors publishing company for your expertise.

Last but not least, to the many individuals who knowingly or unknowingly shared their experiences making this book an important resource – a huge thank you.

Table of Contents

Introduction

massive heart attack - At eighty-one, my dad was dead leaving my mother and I in shock. Dad and Mom decided to go out for dinner to their favorite restaurant. It was a beautiful July evening and upon returning home Dad went into the bedroom, sat down in his chair and screamed for my mother to call an ambulance. However, by the time it arrived it was too late. Walking into the living room, I heard my mother sobbing uncontrollably. Her voice was almost inaudible. She kept saying, "I need to locate my brother. I can't find him."

She wanted me to help locate her brother, my uncle. They had not spoken in fifteen years after inflicting the silent treatment on each other. Now she needed support. Our family was small. We had just lost my brother to cancer three years prior at the age of thirty-five. Losing my Dad was frightening and devastating. It left only my Mother and me. My mom's bond with her brother had been strong through their early adult years and she was now reaching out for him during this devastating time.

As we notified friends of Dad's passing, we frantically tried to locate my mother's brother and his children. After calling the church, town hall, or anyone we could think of, he was nowhere to be found. This was 1990 and the internet wasn't what it is today so that was no help. Then the second shock came thirty years later – when through the internet I finally connected with my cousin. My uncle had died years before. Mom died without being able to say good-bye or telling her brother how much he meant to her. My heart ached for her. How sad!

What happened that caused this silent treatment for so many years? I was determined to investigate what this silent treatment was all about-- the weapon many of us use to cut family and friends out of our lives, which in turn, can remove them from our children's lives as well. Why do we isolate those that are closest to us, putting them and ourselves in a box of silence? Have you received or given the silent treatment to someone? It is damaging, painful and destructive. Why is it important to repair family relationships, friendships, and business relationships where communication has ceased?

This book is a simple uncomplicated look inside the reasons why we use the silent treatment to express our feelings without words and how to reconnect the broken bridge of communication between people that this silence causes.

My goal is to share my struggles and observations with silence as a weapon in relationships, and my suggestions for remedying the situation. My credentials are from personal experience only in observing the abuse caused by the silent treatment. If someone has meaning to you, if you love them, don't let this happen! By being aware of the facts and understanding the situation with an open mind you too, will be able to find the compromise, the open playing field of reuniting broken relationships.

If you picked up this book and peeked inside, you probably have had some experience with the silent treatment – a very powerful, passive form of nonverbal communication. You may recognize yourself or situations where you are wasting precious time, sometimes years, by this destructive withhold of love and friendship. Some give it and others get it. It can carry over to the next generation, causing great emotional pain. It is a toxic behavior without words, confronting the other with passive aggressiveness. Contempt and displeasure can be expressed without giving their target an opportunity to get out of the box they are in and explain or correct their position on the problem. It allows their target to be belittled by the person, controlled, and devalued. With a willingness to view the situation through a different set of circumstances and an open mind set, we can repair the communication and relationship back to love.

As I began my journey, exploring why we silence each other, I was looking strictly in my own backyard. Silence between family and close friends, as well as my own personal encounters with silence, is what makes this topic important to me. As I began to explore the topic something began to happen. Story after story, writings and conversations about broken family relationships popped up out of nowhere. It was like buying a new car that you aren't familiar with. It may be the make or the color you haven't seen before. All of a sudden you see the car everywhere. That is what happened with my writing. My awareness had changed. I began to listen on a deeper level to what was being said by other victims of the silent treatment, to understand the underlying sadness and pain that can be buried for years with broken relationships. I realized that silence and ghosting are a much larger occurrence than most people think about.

Acquaintances who had been in front of me all along shared their stories without ever knowing it because they had a need to talk about their pain and I finally had my ears and heart open to hear them. A business owner in town is now returning to his native country to repair a deep disconnect with his grandmother who had raised him. When his parents divorced, he not only silenced them but his grandmother as well. He has felt guilty for years and has grown enough to have the strength to try to reconcile. Brothers and sisters stopped talking because of anger and jealousy between their spouses, friends, and business colleagues.

I met Sal doing some volunteer work in town. He was always generous with his time giving to whoever needed him. Sal was subjected to the silent treatment because of an assumption his friend had made about him. Did the silencing occur because this person perhaps made a mistake in his judgment about Sal? He tried numerous times to reach out and discuss what happened only to be met with more silence. If they encountered each other in a store, this person ran down another aisle to avoid having to confront Sal. To this day, he honestly, has no idea what caused this abrupt cut off.

I came across Paul Simon's "Sounds of Silence" written over several months between 1963 and 1964. His words are powerful and expressed to me the damage caused by the silent treatment that are still true today.

"The Sound of Silence"
….And in the naked light I saw
Ten thousand people, maybe more
People talking without speaking
People hearing without listening
People writing songs that voices never share
No one dared
Disturb the sound of silence

"Fools," said I, "You do not know
Silence like a cancer grows
Hear my words that I might teach you
Take my arms that I might reach you."
But my words like silent raindrops fell
And echoed in the wells of silence…

It is my hope that my words and the words of the song will make you think about the huge gaps of silence in your own relationships and life and will lead to communication, forgiveness, and reconciliations.

Each of us has the power to explore how to reassess our emotions and separate facts and truth from confusing feelings. Life is short. If you have had a bond with someone and value a relationship, communicating feelings are better than the cold grave silence. A healthy disagreement or argument doesn't mean you don't love the other person. The fear of expressing your point of view should be erased. If your heart is hurting and you feel trapped and unable to reach out, this book is for you. Silence isn't golden and I want to share the insight I have gotten to remedy this and encourage you to take the necessary steps to bridge this sad divide.

I understand this subject may not be popular. I hope it will help with healing families and friendships by removing this festering splinter called silence. If left in, thorns of resentment and hatred can become poison. If left unchallenged it may turn into an irreparable cold indifference and the total death of a relationship.

I hope to shine a light on how we engage in this type of communication, why we use it as a weapon and its abusiveness. The book is divided into three sections that explore what the silent treatment is, why we shut people out of our lives and how positive remedies open up communication and bring back healing and love to both parties.

I convey different viewpoints, backgrounds, and upbringings to show that we are all complicated individuals that need an unconditional open atmosphere where we can see and speak words of encouragement. From *One Day At a Time in Al-Anon*, "Today I pray for the wisdom to build a better tomorrow on the mistakes and experiences of yesterday."

When Silence Isn't Golden is from my heart, hopefully reaching your heart, healing pain and awakening reconciliation for all recipients who have been hurt by the weapons of silence.

Part 1
Recognizing the Silent Treatment

Chapter 1
The Gap of Silence

One day we are talking and engaged in conversation and, suddenly, we are shut out and cut off as if we are on opposite sides of the road, spanning miles of incredible distance. Silence is a strong form of communication that can speak louder than words and can be used as a weapon to control. It is an avoidance of being straight up and saying what you mean and then having to mean what you say. Silence conveys a whole array of emotions from anger to frustration and it is a devastating way to stop communicating with those we love and care for. There is something deeper at play between people than just speaking words. Relationships including marriages racial issues and differences in religious beliefs are other areas that can result in the use of the silent treatment.

There is a big difference between taking a time out and reflecting on a situation and the complete verbal and emotional cut off that is used in the silent treatment. Temporary quietness to get in touch with our thoughts is good. It gives us a chance to align our thoughts and words with our actions. It will not be destructive to the relationship. One of my go-to online counseling resources has this definition of a cooling off period versus the silent treatment. It states "Do not confuse the silent treatment with something known as the 'cooling off period.' The cooling off period is where one person is so angry or disgusted by the other person that they just cannot deal with the situation in that state and need time to calm down before they begin speaking to this person. That's normal and should be allowed in a relationship. Purposely ignoring and refusing to hear or talk to a person is wrong, intentional, manipulative and demonstrates extreme calculation and cruelty on how to hurt another person or even drive them crazy."

My definition of the silent treatment is broad and includes those minimal responses such as um – hum. Or the polite response, "I'll call you". You never get the call and are left wondering why the relationship went dead.

The silent treatment is a behavior that walls you off in your own corner. You are isolated, stuck with pain and hurt that can be passed to future generations, creating sad and damaging outcomes for all. Emotional, spiritual, and physical deterioration occurs in relationships that suffer from the silent treatment.

"The silent treatment, even if it is brief, activates the anterior cingulate cortex-the part of the brain that detects physical pain. The initial pain is the same regardless of whether the exclusion is by strangers, close friends, or enemies." explains Kipling Williams, Professor of Psychology at Purdue University. (https://www.purdue.edu>experts)

The gap of silence to me is defined by any communication where you are intentionally shut off or shut out from being able to respond to a situation and purposely being avoided. You cannot respond in your own defense. It is a safe place to avoid any confrontation. "Excluding and ignoring people, such as giving them the cold shoulder or silent treatment are used to punish or manipulate, and people may not realize the emotional or physical harm that is being done," says Kipling Williams, Professor of Psychology at Purdue University.

My personal experience with silence began in childhood. Not talking when you were angry was passed down from generation to generation in our home. Experiencing this silence was confusing and made me feel isolated. As a young adult the silent treatment was more indirect.

A friend, Sue, once said to me, "I'll call you back, talk later" and a year went by, and I never heard from her. I reached out to her with no response. Her not wanting to air her dirty laundry was the reason she silenced me. We had decided to double-date and go dancing at Bear Mountain. We each took our own cars and decided to meet there at 8 pm. This was a fairly new date for my girlfriend. As we walked into the ballroom, we passed the band.

We were shown to our table and immediately Sue and her date, Will said, "We can't explain, but we have to leave.

Sue said, "I will call you later."

I called her the next day and did not get an answer or hear from her again. I went through all scenarios wondering if they did not want to be with me and my date. Maybe they didn't like where we had gone. I was told later Will was married and his father-in-law was a musician sitting in the front row of the band. To this day I don't know if she knew he was married or was she feeling shame? If we had a chance to talk about the evening a wonderful friendship would not have been destroyed.

I want to know where I stand with another person either good or bad. As a natural communicator I am blessed to be able to put myself out there and tell you who I am and what is going on in my head as well as my heart. I am afraid at times and feel vulnerable when reaching out to someone who has shut our communication down. My first thought is "what did I do to cause it?" I recognize that there is a gap in our communication as well as a gnawing pit in my stomach that says the relationship is in trouble.

I include social media as a way some individuals attempt to accomplish shutting people out of their lives. We fear alienating a close friend or family member when we have an opinion on a subject that we know is different and important to someone else. We unfriend them or stop following them on social media or we misinterpret their sharing of articles, and quickly delete them and don't respond. We don't take the time to understand what they are thinking or feeling, and our interpretation can distort our opinion of them. It leaves a lot of room for assumption and the other person not being able to respond with their truth. I include texting as a tool that fosters the silent treatment. Texting can be very vague. Misconstrued content can leave you lost unless you love texting and keep pressuring the other person for what they meant. Texting has led me to make wrong assumptions and conclusions about people and relationships.

I am a very literal person, and it is easy for me to interpret wording incorrectly. I can get a better read if I can hear your voice or, better yet, see you in person.

This morning my good friend called and said with a bit of sarcasm and humor, "Are you going to get a lot done today?"

I must have sighed and said "hum". She then said "Write". I took it as right, like yeah right. Because we were on the phone, she realized I had taken it wrong and said, "No write." This might not have been clarified if we were texting. If you don't go back and forth in a text to understand what is being said you can make all sorts of assumptions that aren't correct.

The internet is also a place that allows us to post a view that we feel passionate about but is not popular with whom we are sending it to. I personally feel texting and social media are used as a hiding place. It allows a space to express and vent your viewpoint without any direct contact or confrontation. The social media acts as a bridge and safety net for individuals to say what they need to say and remain safe. With the click of a button, they can snooze the opinion that might be coming back on them. Social media can allow you to post anything from sick humor to fake news. In families where there are different opinions especially politics these days, you can be in trouble. I have snoozed a few family members and friends for a while to have them send their opinions to me in messenger or Facebook. Many times, I have wanted to totally block them but what good would the silence of not receiving these posts get me? I would miss all the good ones we share.

My personal opinion is we are losing good, clear communication skills with social media. Without them, it is difficult to repair conflicts. Social media allows us to assume and create our own story unless we are clear about what the other person is saying to us. It helps perpetuate the "Silent Treatment."

There are many reasons why lack of communication and silence occurs between individuals. I believe most people lack constructive communication skills such as negotiating, compromising, and above all, listening without an agenda. If you are determined to win, be right, control and be inflexible you will most likely partake of the silent treatment and shut others down verbally. Rather than listen objectively and with an open heart you will selectively choose what you hear and what you will fit into your winning story. You will be interested in validating what matters to you.

If we don't give thought to the importance of those we care about with love, our emotions and traits we possess will run the show. Many traits get us in this mess and help drive our rigid, uncompromising behavior. It takes guts to have difficult conversations if you want relationships to continue. Taking an inventory of some of the negative traits which cause us to use the silent treatment might give us a start as to why we cut someone out of our life. A few of the negative traits include:

- ignoring others
- judging
- belittling
- assuming
- criticizing
- stubbornness
- vindictiveness
- inflexibility
- negativity

- low self esteem
- fear
- pride
- thwarted expectations
- anger
- impatience
- suspicion
- jealousy
- comparing
- grudges
- resentment
- retaliation

If we normalize the causes of the silent treatment and shut people out, it will become easier to default to these behaviors. Realizing and understanding something about others' lives, their unhappiness, pain, compulsions and addictions will help us understand them and avoid reacting to everything they do. Sometimes what isn't said is as important as what is said.

Many emotions and thoughts go through our head and get exchanged every day. I have decided to think about that rhyme, "Sticks and Stones will break my bones, but words will never hurt me." Words do hurt us, that is, if we allow them to. I am honestly trying to practice what I preach and always trying to take a look at the bigger and whole picture of a situation – not my small corner. The real trouble and conflict begin when we stop communication and begin ghosting.

Ghosting is the new term used for the silent treatment or stonewalling, originating in the early

2000's. Whether we are the rejected or the ones giving the stonewalling it is passive – aggressive and causes emotional pain and abuse. This reminds me of a phone conversation I had with my grandson, Ryan. He began to tell me about his girlfriend, Amanda and was explaining it was the start of their senior year and they were in a tough position. They wanted to spend time together but did not want to dive into a deep relationship because they were going to attend different colleges. That sounded like a wise decision to me. Then he said he had ghosted her for a while and asked "Gram, do you know what ghosting is?" He said, "You probably don't."

I got the gist of the word but said "not really." When I looked up the term I went "Oh my gosh, this is what I am writing my book about."

Ryan went on to explain that he and Amanda had gone on a mission trip to Houston, Texas with their youth group and found themselves sitting in front of an industrial fan on a very hot night, fighting the heat and talking for hours. It was the first time Ryan got to find out who his girlfriend was. Things felt different, "We weren't just dating we were friends that got along so well" to quote Ryan. "We were in the best spot we had ever been." Then the pandemic hit.

Ryan had been troubled by depression and anxiety for two years and he finally felt he had dug himself out emotionally only to have COVID-19 put him in lock down. He stated it made him feel everything had been taken away from him. He didn't know what to do with his life and needed "time to himself as the pandemic took over the world." This was the point he ghosted Amanda. Ryan and Amanda didn't have a conversation that it was over. They both just went their separate ways.

The relationship began to rekindle when the pandemic caused them to return to their parents' home in the same town. Fate stepped in and ended up with them meeting in a public parking lot next to McDonalds, talking and sharing many feelings and emotions. They had an honest conversation about how they felt with COVID-19 screwing up their first year of college and their relationship. According to Ryan, "We decided we wanted to rekindle the fire and try things out again."

This was a situation where the feelings were present even though they had stopped speaking. Someone has to reach out and jumpstart the conversation if it is to be rekindled. We don't know what outcomes can transpire from our actions and words. If you are ghosting and feel compelled to reach out to the other person – pick up the phone if you can or, at least, reach out with a text. Life is so short and so much pain and emotional suffering can be spared if we walk across that bridge of silence. It is better to remove a splinter than to have it left in for years or a lifetime festering and causing pain.

Good luck Ryan and thank you for bringing me up to date on ghosting, the new definition of the silent treatment - same treatment but different generations.

Silence isn't golden when:
- We cut and shut people off to protect our fragile selves
- Awareness of our actions is not recognized

- We use social media to push our opinions on someone else
- We stop communicating and talking using text or social media instead
- Our reaction to a situation determines our outcome
- We don't watch our choice of words
- We think distance separates people – silence does

Chapter 2
Who is Shooting the Arrow?

We are all capable of both giving the silent treatment and receiving it. My journey of researching this with friends, family and acquaintances has substantiated my beliefs. Quite a few of the people I interviewed shared their views admitting they were the victims of the silent treatment and were also the perpetrators. When I decided to investigate this behavior, I thought very few people ever experienced the actual hurt and emotional upset that I had with the silent treatment. I was tempted to scrub the whole notion of this being of importance to anyone but myself and my own wounds.

All types of individuals with different personalities engage in the silent treatment for different reasons. If the person is truly vindictive and acting out of malice you are probably stuck living with it until there is a change of heart or point of view on their part. Issues like depression, addictions, and mental problems also trigger the hiding out and silence by others. They are likely feeling trapped and isolated themselves which is also what you feel with this silence. Discrepancies in our belief systems, assumptions based on past experiences and not knowing or accepting what the truth of a situation might be, can all make us feel specifically and purposefully an injured party. Maybe so but it all depends on each individual's sensitivity and old tapes. You can be the person who shot the arrow or the one who got hit by it. My view is that both parties have been affected by this silent treatment and the receiver is forced to engage in it.

Self- preservation can be a cause to withdraw from someone. Depression and anger were the cause of having to give the silent treatment to a neighbor. I had just moved into a lovely development in Pennsylvania. All the neighbors had introduced themselves including Pamela. She was about fifty-five and had been a nurse. We were both dog lovers, so we had an immediate connection. I usually saw her out in the yard by herself. Her husband, Chuck, who was a retired cop in New Jersey, was rarely seen with her. One afternoon Pamela came over for coffee and poured her heart out about the abuse she was getting from her husband and how she suffered from his depression and anger issues. Her personality and moods also were a little erratic. One day she was angry, yelling at the dogs, and then the next day, everything was fine.

Several weeks later she had her husband signed into the psychiatric floor at the local hospital for her safety. Her assumption was he would remain there and receive a psychiatric evaluation. However, he was able to sign himself out. One day I received a phone call from Pamela and then from her daughter asking if I would drive her to Jersey before he returned home. I thought we would meet him coming up the road on his way home. Honestly, I was afraid for my safety and told her I could not do that and suggested she call the authorities if she needed help or a family member. She became very angry and slammed the phone down on me. Pamela then called another neighbor, Marge, with the same request and received the same answer. "I can't do that." Her daughter did come to pick her up with her mother's five dogs before Chuck got home.

In a matter of months, he died at the age of sixty and she returned back to their home in Pennsylvania. She would not speak to any of us in the neighborhood or even wave. Possibly it was embarrassment or was it latent anger because we weren't able to help her. This was a situation where we both were the givers and the receivers of the silence. You never know what causes a person to react. For me, it was not getting involved in an unsafe situation. We never spoke after that.

Silence is used to run away from speaking our truth out of fear and avoiding certain emotional outcomes. When we are complicit with the silent treatment, we isolate ourselves on one side of the bridge. These deep feelings we have buried are like suppressed "old tapes" that interfere with our ability to process facts properly. These old tapes are the repetitive stories we keep playing in our head, either imagined or real hurts. We take refuge in silence and create a place to hide out hoping to remain loyal to family and friends. It takes courage to speak out at times making your truth known rather than running to a safe corner where you and the other person can't explore a viewpoint – least of all be able to defend it.

Locking ourselves off in silence isn't always intentional. Sometimes people are confined emotionally due to the loneliness that comes from aging, sickness, or a cultural experience, such as with a language barrier. Heartaches and feeling obsolete and discarded can cause confusion and some people decide to retreat and cut off communication to protect themselves – hiding behind the closed door of silence they alone are creating.

Life occasionally throws us things we can't always resolve and retreating provides a false sense of emotional preservation. Using the silent treatment for protection by disengaging from a person or situation temporarily gives you the safe haven you seek. My interviews with people who are the givers or receivers of this silence live with isolation. Most individuals ponder what happened, even after years of not speaking, with some remorse, a choice they made and now live with. The fortunate people will recognize what is happening and be able to mend silence not only for themselves but for future generations.

I sent out an email to my writing group asking if anyone would care to share stories on the silent treatment. Mary gladly shared. She was the giver of the silent treatment. She had been actively involved in various local charities and was very giving of her time, especially the United Way. She was liked by everyone who worked with her. If something needed to be done, Mary was your girl.

Apparently one woman, Amy, constantly came to Mary for help and then would give her the cold shoulder when she no longer needed her. Mary would reach out to her only to have her calls or texts go unanswered. This behavior went on for several years and Mary just accepted it for what it was. Many months had elapsed, and Mary decided it was time to stop being the doormat all the time. A large project came up and out of the blue, the phone rang with Amy saying, "Hi, how are you?" Mary knew she was receiving the call because she needed help with the project.

This time Mary said "hello" and decided enough was enough. She made an excuse to get off the phone and avoided Amy's calls after that. There are givers and takers in this world and Mary had been taken by Amy for the last time. Mary said, she has no regrets that she gave her the silent treatment.

Our country is more culturally diverse than ever, and the misunderstandings that happen due to language barriers or unfamiliar customs can create a huge gap between people. I first met my neighbor, Christa when I moved into my home across the street from her. I had been told by other neighbors that she did not speak to anybody except the lady Pat who lived next door to her. Christa came to the United States from Germany at the age of fourteen. I had taken German in high school and remembered a few words. Upon meeting her I said hello in German and that brought a smile to her face, and she slowly accepted me. She loved my dogs and could relate to animals better than humans.

Christa is an example of retreating behind the wall of silence. She is of European heritage and lived by herself after her husband died. She did have stepchildren who spoke to her in her native language, German. Well into her nineties she still cut her own grass and loved working in her garden. She never missed a hairdresser appointment to take care of her beautiful white hair. Doctor visits were more of a challenge. She didn't like most doctors. The one she disliked the most was German and could speak to her in her native tongue.

Christa's main concern or possible excuse for not conversing was her belief she did not have a grasp of the English language. The neighbors all thought she spoke English very well. She was always capable of relating her problems and concerns in English to repairmen and even had been an owner of a deli in New York years ago. She was very good at writing and reading English and paid her own bills. She cooked, shopped, loved eating in fine restaurants and visiting the casino occasionally. Christa was very capable of telling you what she didn't like or want. So was she isolating and living a life of non-communication today with friends and neighbors who have cared for her over the years?

If she was in her yard and neighbors come out to speak with her, she would run in the house. If we came out and waved she would run inside and peek through her curtains and watch us. If neighbors and friends were lucky enough to call her and she picked up the phone you will have a partial conversation with her as long as you didn't ask her too many questions.

Christa formed her own wall of silence that inflicted isolation on herself by her belief systems and her fears. I do believe she was never a big communicator, but friends and family could always draw her out and she enjoyed life. I question whether it was the aging process with visual and hearing challenges, or did she become what she always believed she was an obsolete person in a new country? Were the old tapes running in the background –"I can't speak well, I don't think the neighbors like me," Or was she just mad at life?

It was a very sad ending. The more negative and isolated she became, friends and family stayed away believing she was taking care of her business as usual. All she wanted was to stay in her home with her belongings until the end. She ended up in a nursing home and died. Isolation is devastating for some even when they choose it. When we isolate, we only have our own truths and realities which may not be accurate, especially as we age. The more we retreat we lose our way. Stay connected.

Silence isn't golden when:
- We run on old tapes or the "stories we tell ourselves"
- We isolate from others and cut off communication
- We close off communication based on assumptions of how we view a situation and our discrepancies and beliefs.

Chapter 3
Silence Living in Our Conscious and Subconscious

There are two types of reasons why the silent treatment is given – conscious and subconscious awareness and both are equally damaging. Conscious awareness comes from actively choosing to participate in the silent treatment. If you are on the receiving end of being cut off, you know it is happening. You realize it is more than just taking a time out. You have been shut out. Perhaps it was a swift avoidance of communication and contact. Phone calls were not responded to, and notes and texts ignored. The new term for the silent treatment is ghosting. You may have reached them on the phone and received a "Can I call you back later? I am in the middle of something." Later never came. Feelings run through your head. What have I done? What caused this to happen and then the question, "Can I do something to remedy this?" Should I keep asking what the problem is or just wait? The silence is ringing louder than any words at this point.

If you are the giver of the silent treatment and consciously and actively using it towards someone, you have a pretty good idea of what you are doing and why. You have the awareness. You are shutting the person out of your life because they have hurt you or you are angry with them for a particular reason, situation, or a misunderstanding. You feel strongly that you don't want to communicate or be around them. We may also silence someone and grow apart because we aren't able to cope with their mental issues, job choices, or geographical changes. Money is a big trigger as was with a young man and his sister.

Connor's mother passed away in 2018. His sister, Sue, was the executrix of his mother's will. Sue had never liked Connor's wife and felt she was a spendthrift that would deplete Connor's inheritance in a heartbeat. Two years went by, and Sue had divided the possessions except for some stocks and bonds that she locked in a trust. Connor asked Sue to finalize the will and the request fell on deaf ears. Finally, Connor's wife convinced him it was done maliciously because Sue didn't like her, and they should get a lawyer and take his sister to court. They did just that and won the case. Connor received his money which now his wife mostly controls. Connor and Sue no longer speak. Sue has totally cut him and his wife off by giving them the silent treatment.

I can't say that Connor and his sister were close emotionally. However, they cared about each other as family. Any support they could possibly give each other, as well as the sharing of future memories, came to an end with the silent treatment. They weren't able to overcome the bitterness and move beyond what happened. I don't think either one of them saw the future implications this lawsuit would have on their relationship and families.

Annie, a very open and spiritual lady, was willing to share her difficult childhood with me. She had many years of turmoil with an emotionally sick mother who suffered from multiple personality disorders including obsessive compulsive disorder (OCD) which manifested itself in compulsive cleaning. Her mother's violent mood swings caused her father to be absent from the home to not trigger fighting and upheaval for his children.

Annie's mother silenced her at the age of nineteen by kicking her out of the house. Her mother constantly criticized her for not being enough even though she was a straight "A" student. She was blessed to be able to move in with her aunt and grandmother. Annie had two siblings who were still in the volatile home and being verbally and physically abused.

Annie's relationship with her dad was another story. She and her siblings had been brainwashed by her mother into thinking that her father was the problem. Acting on these incorrect assumptions and anger, she decided to turn on her dad and use the silent treatment to distance herself from the hurt and pain she felt. She sporadically made attempts to speak to her mom and check on her siblings. Annie eventually married and had a daughter. She wanted her daughter to have a relationship with her grandfather. After years of not communicating with her dad, she decided to re-establish a bridge of communication and he was receptive to her outreach. Her first question to him was, "Why did you abandon us?"

His reply was "to keep peace for you."

By taking that step to reach and build that bridge back, she and her daughter were able to establish a good relationship before he died.

Subconscious awareness is different. Old tapes and old stories are running in the back of your mind and may skew the way you perceive a situation at a particular time. A situation may bring up and trigger a hurt or angry feeling. If we aren't conscious of the cause we can react by cutting off a friend or family member because we have allowed an emotion we aren't recognizing, let alone understanding, to push them away with silence.

If I don't hear you, I can forget you are there and I won't have to deal with the feelings and the discomfort of facing sensitive emotions and issues. If I shut you out, I don't have to deal with the larger problems underlying the silence that has layered up. Silence is a symptom of what has been ignored and can't be reckoned with.

Many times, we aren't aware of how much we are being run by our subconscious mind. I met a forty-year-old woman at church named Karen, who shared her experiences with the silent treatment. As a child she stated, "I wasn't liked by most of the kids in my class." She went on to say she also had a very critical father who constantly criticized her growing up. For protection she would isolate from her friends and not speak to them unless she was forced to. It became an automatic response that carried over into her adult relationships. Any confrontation or criticism caused her to shut you out. This continued until she realized the subconscious pain from the past was running her life. Other than stating it was a relationship in college that triggered her seeking therapy she was being run by past emotions and memories. Silence was the invisible wall she used to cope and prevent herself from hurt. Once she realized the role her subconscious mind was doing to her, she said "I was finally able to consciously take steps to heal myself and rebuild some old relationships I had destroyed."

Sometimes it takes years for subconscious tapes and feelings to awaken and make sense. We exist in blind denial of what is happening emotionally until this behavior is recognized. At this point we can look objectively at what the situation was and why it happened. The process of acknowledging the old tapes and hurts may take years to surface into something we can perceive. Life's events, assumptions and being able to get off the treadmill of life can be starting points for this new conscious realization. Retirement, a confining illness, job changes such as giving up your career to stay home with children possibly slows you down enough to think and view life in a different way.

I interviewed a church member who was cut off by her mother-in-law, Rose, the first Christmas of their marriage. Rose had been invited for Christmas dinner to Ray and her daughter-in-law Jane's home. Rose never notified them that she decided she would not join them. She just never showed up. She went to her sister's home instead. After this incident, Rose never spoke to her daughter–in–law again. No matter how often Jane reached out through phone calls and notes, still silence. Her husband, Ray, would go to his mother's house and try to mend fences. It would result in an argument, and he would leave. Encouraged by his wife, Jane, he continued to keep in touch with visits and phone calls. He just would not bring up any conversation having to do with his wife.

The silence continued until Rose died twenty-five years later. When Ray's mother was in the hospital, his last conversation with her was "I am not sorry I have ignored your wife all these years. I did not want you to marry her because I did not think she was good for you since she was an only child."

Rose's assumption of who she thought Ray's wife was and her anger towards him for marrying her, prevented Rose from getting to know her daughter-in-law and enjoying a loving relationship with both of them. Non-communication with Ray's mother was more of a relief for Ray and Jane's relationship. Rose created severe stress and anxiety for both of them. The silence was made easier to maintain because Ray and Jane had no children. If there were children involved, would the situation be different? Parents will sacrifice for their children whether or not they want to. There is no guarantee that she would want a relationship, but Ray and Jane would have done what they could to make it happen.

I began consciously contemplating the silent treatment that began with my dad passing away and not being able to locate the small family my mother and I had left. I wanted to shield her from the loneliness and heartache of not being able to reconnect with her brother. It took me until the last few years to realize why I let it bother me or gave it a thought. Subconsciously, I had experienced the silent cut-off and disconnect as a child starting with my mother. It was a real wow moment when the subconscious memories and feelings became a conscious vivid reality. For me, I recognized the connection of the subconscious to the conscious, the day after my dad's funeral when my mother asked to find her brother. I remember the triggering event so clearly even now forty-five years later.

Awareness of the silent treatment is the first step. As a child, I couldn't process what was happening. As an adult it took that ah-ha moment to shine a spotlight connecting the conscious and subconscious. My Mom also was parenting from her old tapes of being ignored as a child with the silent treatment.

"I hate you" I screamed and then burst into tears. These were the words of a four-year-old child to her mother. Then came the punishment of the silent treatment towards me. As I look back now as an adult, the silence seemed to last in my mind for weeks. It was probably only for a few days. I was shut out and cut off from being able to apologize and isolated from the love and communication I needed from her.

Mom suffered from anxiety and depression and self-medicated with alcohol and periodically prescription medications for chronic ailments. My dad traveled for a living and was only home on the weekends which left my mom to run the house and be responsible for the care of my brother and me as well. Severe stress kept her on edge and I constantly took every opportunity, I could think of, to get her love and attention I so craved. Pressuring her for this at the wrong time brought on tension, anger and then the wrath of silence.

I was a perceptive child and on days her voice was sharp and her extra tight grip on my hand conveyed I was not only annoying her but getting on her last nerve. I knew, at that point, she was not hearing a word I might be saying to her. Total frustration on my part as a four-year- old child, not being heard, made me feel isolated and not listened to and then out would come the anger I was feeling. "I hate you" was my way of getting attention.

I was too young to be able to rationalize or understand what was transpiring on a conscious level with the silent treatment. However, I had absorbed it subconsciously. I accepted this silence as part of the day and my relationship with her. It was a practice she had used over the years with other family members. It was not the kind of attention I wanted. I would beg for her to forgive me, constantly trying to make amends by asking her if I could help her set the table or anything to end the silence and the disconnection I felt from her. She dismissed any interaction or apology and spoke only short sentences such as go to bed or other (commands), she felt I needed to hear. She just wouldn't hear me.

Then the lights came on the moment my dad passed away. Mom was once again alone to care for herself, and she frantically tried to reach out for her brother – whom she had cut off years before. She could not locate him. Every attempt she made failed. He never responded to her or attempted to contact her back. My heart ached for her, but it also ached for me as well. I understood that she was experiencing the silent treatment in return.

This was a real ah-ha moment for me. I felt like I was punched in the stomach. The conscious experience of seeing what was happening with my mother connected. I understood instantly the emotions of fear and loneliness I had experienced as a child subconsciously. The receiver of the silent treatment this time was my mother, and it was given to her by her brother.

It was the catalyst of awareness showing how destructive silence is when used as a weapon, and how families perpetuate this behavior from one generation to another.

Silence isn't golden when we don't question:
- Avoidance
- Buried anger
- Old tapes
- Not listening
- Why we are holding anger

Chapter 4
The Silent Generation

The silent treatment is often carried from one generation to the next. Why and how does this occur? My belief is that the old tapes and beliefs are not recognized and we have a hard time coping with situations and experiences that we are afraid of facing. We also mimic what we saw and absorbed as children in homes that used silence as a weapon. If the way we experienced unpleasant situations and confrontation was to put hands over our ears saying, "I don't hear you", the child will not consciously recognize how inappropriate this is as a way to handle the situation. Subconsciously, it probably is stored as an old tape and the behavior will be continued. My hope is it will be acknowledged that silence exists and is not the remedy to a problem.

I interviewed a woman named Gloria, who spoke about the silence between her dad's family and her mother. They never accepted her mom due to her ethnic background and therefore ghosted her. Gloria's aunts ostracized her family and never spoke to her mom. This impacted the relationship into the next generation. Since they never spoke, Gloria never met all of her cousins. Evidently, unbeknownst to Gloria, the aunts compared Gloria to her cousin, Joyce, who was the same age. Joyce was always the fair-haired girl. An uncle by marriage to Joyce and Gloria who was also ostracized by the family was able to get both girls a summer job on Wall St in New York.

After a week, Joyce quit and left to go work at Shop Rite while Gloria worked on Wall Street all four years while in college. Both of them went into education and became elementary school teachers in the same town. The next time Gloria saw Joyce was fifteen years later when she became an Assistant Principal at her school. Gloria had hoped they could develop a relationship, but Joyce ghosted her at every turn and never spoke about the other cousins. Even though there were two other cousins who were her age, to this day she has never met them. It was sad because Gloria was an only child and could have used their friendship, fun and support in her early years and as an adult.

There is a lot that goes into unpacking your motivations for giving or receiving the silent treatment and using it as a weapon with family members. It might start by questioning how important this person is to you or your family. Is it worth taking a more objective look at the situation and asking yourself why you are cutting the person off? If you are the one receiving the silent treatment, why have they cut you off or why is this individual isolated? Should you take a moment to question those childhood old tapes that exist from observed and learned behavior?

We absorb what we see and listen to as well as the language of silence. As children we don't know this behavior can be inappropriate for the circumstance and would be better addressed in a different way. Silence is destructive and debilitating.

The silent treatment can be passed down from one generation to another and from one family member to another. The loss of family connection is devastating. Siblings do not speak to each other; cousins do not know each other and grandparents are estranged from grandchildren. This happened in my family.

My grandmother, Nana and her sister, Mary, were very close. She had a daughter Rose and a son, Jon who were two years apart. Mary had a daughter, Carrie, who also was my godmother. They were close in age and traveled to Europe together as teenagers with their mothers and enjoyed each other's families and successes. Rose, Jon and Carrie, cousins that were bonded in love and fun for years, until a slow erosion took place and one day they turned their backs on each other and never spoke, each bridged in silence. What happened to cause the break in the relationship?

The first break was Rose and Jon having a falling out with their cousin, Carrie. Carrie had lost patience with both Rose and Jon's family drama. Depression had caused much sadness in both their homes due to sickness with alcoholism in Rose's home, my mother, and depression in my uncle's home. Both had suffered a childhood with a father dying young. I believe they never resolved their grief. Old stories were never questioned. My grandmother's money and physical possessions came into play when she passed away. Carrie never came to the funeral nor spoke again to her cousins. Apparently, they did not think she deserved to be included in my grandmother's estate.

On the day of my grandmother's funeral we went to lunch, my family and only my uncle Jon. We made small talk trying to normalize what was happening. The next day my mom and uncle divided the few things she owned and that was the last time I saw my uncle. He handled the estate, and I am speculating after a few fights over money, my mother wrote him off in silence and buried anger.

Relationships between cousins and siblings dissolved quickly that day, erasing thirty years of love, memories, and sweet family times they enjoyed as children supposedly because of money and possessions. Was there a deeper-rooted cause? They all had problems verbalizing feelings, buried anger, lack of being able to confront the pain and speak their truth with love and understanding. They ran instead.

Carrie was the first to exhibit the silent treatment. Was she afraid or incapable of sharing and expressing her feelings or had she been so hurt by her cousins' behavior that enough was enough? Was my grandmother an excuse to end the relationship? My Godmother, the person I looked up to as a loving family member and mentor picked up, moved, and died with not one more word to any of us. Silence and no contact created a big void in my life. I tried to reach out to her with no success. Her actions and mindset just erased us. This was the first cousin episode.

My mother, Rose, was an editorial assistant for a large nursing magazine and her brother, Jon, was an executive in corporate America. The silent treatment between my mother and her brother was based in rivalry over money, buried bitterness and jealousy.

Was my grandmother also being used as the excuse for them to part in silence? Obviously, all of the above had been festering for a long time. Finances were a big issue as well as, who did more for her which brought assumptions, judgments, anger, and family pressure into play. Jealousy and thwarted expectations between brother and sister questioned what each should receive monetarily. The spouses of these two, my Dad and Aunt also played into this with hostility causing extra pressure. My grandmother's death was the end of this relationship as well.

Mom and her brother never saw each other again or spoke and neither did my cousins and me. As children we had special memories of happy family times together, holiday traveling, sleepovers etc. These family times were especially enjoyable to us as kids because it broke up the tensions we were feeling at home with parents with depression.

Now that Rose and Jon did not speak or see each other what happened to us cousins that had been so close? We followed what we saw and absorbed as kids and did not communicate as well. I know for myself, I would have felt I was betraying my family if I tried to reach out to them. By the time my dad died, and my mother attempted to reach out to her brother it was too late. It was impossible to locate and find her brother. I, as well, could not reach my cousins. Thirty years later I found my one cousin, Jack's phone number, on the internet and my phone call was well received when I called him. Since then, I have also seen two of my cousins occasionally. All the closeness and time that we had as children was lost and had grown apart. This saddens me greatly as it can't be regained.

My cousins are more resigned to the fact that what occurred between the generations happened. There are three of them and only the middle one has the same sensitivity I do emotionally. Sadly, I see no reconciliation at this point for my cousins and my family.

I ended up being the fortunate one. I kept a lot of memories alive in my head. My mother had also left me a set of diaries documenting our childhood and there were wonderful recollections of happy, fun times with both families. This was a gift for us. After thirty years I met with my cousins in Florida. We had a wonderful dinner together and both had brought pictures and letters. I only stay in touch with my middle cousin, Jack. The younger one isn't interested in rekindling the relationship. Perhaps, too much time was lost. The oldest cousin does not talk much with his brother or sister. Silence perpetuated.

According to Jack, the day my Uncle Jon died, Jack's older brother went over to his dad's house, took a few possessions, and never looked back. My cousin has attempted to reach out to him. They live close to one another, and Jack has stopped by to see him, greeted cordially and then another period of silence. Maybe it is worth taking time to think about what caused this.

In this case, generations repeat the same behavior. Just as my uncle closed the door that October afternoon, so did his one son on his own siblings. If this gap of silence remains and no one attempts to cross it who will ever question what caused it or why there is no attempt to remedy it.

My belief is, in our culture, we ignore the pain of silence. Life keeps us busy rushing from place to place with work and stuff, which distracts us and provides a shield obscuring our vision and awareness. It helps numb our feelings. We can sit back in blind denial. The internet allows harsh words to fly across the airwaves and some hide behind this as a shield as well.

What caused my family to disconnect for me only became clear once I was an adult and I could gain perspective and awareness. I had experienced being given the silent treatment from my mother. I consider myself the lucky one to have recognized how the silent treatment affected our family through the generations. I have been blessed to have an open mind on most issues and attempt to view a situation from my perspective as well as theirs. As a young child this was not possible.

As an adult, I could see both my mother and uncle were products of being exposed to the silent treatment along with the depression they both had. Their father was sick from cancer and died at an early age. Their mother, my grandmother Nana was woman of few words who struggled with the English Language and ran a rooming house in New York. She was a sweet, kind, loving woman who constantly worked to keep a roof over everyone's head. My mom and uncle basically had to raise themselves until they married. As the years went on, unfortunately, my Grandmother was perceived as a problem in both families and became an excuse for all unresolved and buried issues between my mother and her brother.

After she died my mother and brother continued their stonewalling behavior. Why? Did any of them realize what was happening and by speaking they could get a better outcome?

My belief was the bond between my mother and her brother was extremely tight, but they had no skills when it came to confrontation and resolving painful emotional conflicts. That was the end of the relationship between my mom, her brother and family ties to our cousins, aunts, and uncles. By not acknowledging the damage and pain caused by avoidance you can wonder for years. Was it you, your family, your in-laws? Preserving unity in families is important and worth questioning if the silent treatment has been used in your generational family. Our relationships are not only about ourselves.

Silence isn't golden when:
- There is family pressure
- Assumptions
- Thwarted expectations

Part 2
The Damages of Silence

Chapter 5
The Emotional Toll of Not Speaking

Not speaking is a passive way to send our message that we are displeased with the other person and to avoid direct confrontation and emotional pain. Emotionally, silence is an easier approach to convey anger, jealousy, and judgment. Do we think this is also helping us avoid our own pain? Are we consumed with taking care of ourselves? What about the little nagging voice inside our heads? We know that spoken words can incite emotions that are not always pleasant, and we aren't up to the challenge. It takes guts to have those difficult conversations and confront the person as well as the problem. So instead, we choose silence as a way to consciously or subconsciously push someone's buttons remotely. It's uncomfortable for both the silencer and the silenced one. Without communication the problem is left to assumptions. You are leaving the other person wondering what happened to cause the problem and was it their fault.

Silence rears its ugly head as protection for ourselves or to punish others. If you are on the receiving end of the silence, you can interpret this style of communication as hurtful, you can feel that you are being punished, and even abused. Silence speaks as loud as words. *One Day at a Time in Al-anon* says "God help me to know that silence, like speech, can reflect my inner feelings." If we have experienced silence as a punishment or seen it in our families, it feels like a way to handle our differences. Old tapes run our present circumstances. We may not even realize why we do it.

We choose silence for many reasons. We can justify holding on to old hurts and bitterness we possess towards others. It is easier to justify the stories we tell ourselves. It protects us from emotional negative feedback and verbal retaliation. We can send a strong message without having a face-to-face confrontation. We are seeking safety behind this silence from our fears. Fear and silence create suspicion of others' motives towards us. Fear and put downs can make us run and seek protection from those who are not happy with us as well as allow us to be punished by them with crushing silence. They have locked us away in a box with their view of the situation and the lid is crammed on tight. Silence is a double-edged sword. It is either a blessing for those that choose to hide behind the silence or a punishment for those trapped by it.

We often don't take the time to form our thoughts and think before we speak. We put ourselves out on a ledge and don't know how to come back. If we are reactive, not listening and speak on impulse, we can back ourselves into a corner. A few moments spent taking a deep breath before the words come spilling out of our mouth can give us a little time to ask ourselves the question, "Is this really what I want to say?" In those few moments we determine how the relationship might end up. Often from guilt and shame we will start to feel sorry for what happened.

Then what? If we want to rectify the relationship, we might be the ones that have to reach out and make the first gesture of communication. This is not easy, and some people have admitted they don't know how to come back after hiding out in silence.

Sometimes we go so far out on a ledge that we really don't know how to come back to the one we silenced and open the conversation. Both of us are stuck in limbo at that point. The silenced person wonders why they aren't talking and the person who can't reach out is wondering why they can't come back and talk.

Maybe we are not ready to surrender the story we have been telling ourselves. We continue to invent excuses so we can continue our defensive behavior. Without coming back to the table and communicating, how do we remedy the hostilities?

I met Tom on an electrical call he made to my home. Tom was a general contractor and I had found his name in the phone book. As he worked, we started chatting and I asked him if he would do some private work for my elderly neighbor, Christa. His reply was "No, I have learned I am just one spoke in the wheel." I told him I understood he didn't want to take on extra work, but his remark went deeper than that. It began by speaking and words.

I am an approachable person so people, I meet on the street will start telling me their stories. I don't have to solicit them. It was springtime and I was sitting in the lawn chair when Tom finished his work. As he was cleaning up, he began talking and telling me about his life. Tom's background was old tapes filled with hurt from family and relationships. He was a fifty-year-old Vietnam vet who suffered from post-traumatic stress syndrome (PTSD). He was divorced and estranged from his children. He felt he was being taken advantage of at work. He was depressed and disillusioned because he felt things were not going his way.

Tom bounced back and forth in our friendship over five years, often disappearing, not answering phone calls, not calling, and then the silence. Unexpectedly, with much nervousness in his voice, he would call and be remorseful for not being in touch. After one or two calls he would be gone again. This was his pattern of dealing with relationships that became too close and had too much emotion.

This pattern continued with many people in his life until he became terminally ill at fifty-five. He was finally ready to admit he didn't know how to reach out and remedy the silence after these painful periods of time. He had no idea of how to come back to our friendship. My advice was to just come back, override the fear and take the leap. Sometimes it's as simple as beginning with "Hi, how are you doing?"

Finally, Tom was able to see what he was doing and what he had lost by silence. Yes, he still reverted to this behavior when conversations got too emotional for him, but he would pick the phone up if you called him and talk without being reactive. He would text or call you to just let you know he was there. Tom also began to listen, maybe for the first time in his life.

Silence is reinforced through old tapes and habits, old hurts, thwarted expectations, and fear. As Tom's illness progressed, he was thankful he could reunite with all his closest relationships including his children. He passed away having made peace and creating harmony with those around him. Fortunately, he was not too late in reaching out to those who meant so much to him. When we step into the other person's shoes and live in and experience their point of view, our emotional compass shifts from self-preservation to common solidarity.

I remember putting my hands over my ears and chanting the sticks and stones rhyme and saying, "I can't hear you," to my mother. If I can't hear you, I won't be hurt by your words or feelings towards me. I will run away to silence and not face judgment, criticism or feeling attacked.

This is a learned childish response that many of us carry into adulthood. As a child, words being hurled at us can be very traumatic depending on who threw them and how close we are and value this person. Running away and not speaking may be a learned response from childhood. If we continue to handle our confrontations and differences in this manner, we will cut ourselves off from a lot of love. If the lens we look through shuts closed every time we are challenged by what we don't want to hear or face in life we are stuck with a very narrow immature view of what the relationship could have been.

The silent treatment is a behavior that shuts you off from real loving and close relationships. I personally would have experienced a very different relationship with my mother if my defenses hadn't been up since childhood. It took me time to understand that the silence didn't mean she didn't love me. As a child I had been programmed by silence into believing that my viewpoints and opinions meant nothing. Not speaking helped me avoid judgment and criticism. Fortunately, with the help of good friends as role models and some excellent teachers in grade school, I found my voice. You will never get satisfaction of growing a relationship unless both individuals are vulnerable enough to speak their truth and let each other know what's going on in their heads. Being distant won't bring you closer. In our last meaningful conversation together, my mother asked, "We all loved each other but what went wrong?" My heart broke for her.

"There are many families whose systematic way of functioning is to not speak about issues, emotions, and opinions, explains Allan Schwartz, a PhD and licensed clinical social worker with a practice in both Colorado and New York City. "In such families when there is any sign of disagreement everyone "shuts down" or "stuffs it." "Stuffing it" has to do with keeping thoughts and feelings to oneself so as not to hurt the feelings of other people in the family." Schwartz says, "In these "stuffy families," conflict is labeled as dangerous and harmful. Emphasis and value are placed on silence about anything that might be deemed controversial. Each family member works hard to protect the feelings and well-being of the other members. However, this comes at a great cost to everyone in the group."

It is devastating especially when you are young to be disappointed or criticized. Yes, the words matter or lack of words that should be spoken to clarify a situation. Our thoughts on an issue are not always clear and if we sit in silence without speaking, they can become a distorted story we tell ourselves. We create our own version rather than exploring the real reason something happened, definitely a limited version of the situation.

Fortunately for me, friendships I cultivated as an adult helped me learn about myself through the sharing of their thoughts and experiences. Adult Children of Alcoholics was another vehicle which helped me see a more honest and realistic view of myself. Without feedback we are stuck in our own reality. Therapy can also be helpful. Schwartz recommends these types of therapies for families that have stuffed it.

- Family therapy can be extremely helpful in helping families identify and change their patterns of communication. Rather than focus on changing the behavior of a single person, the family therapist concentrates on how the entire family system functions with the purpose of enabling that system to learn healthier and more adaptive ways of communicating and relating to one another.
- Psychodynamic individual therapy can be geared towards the family or the individual. In working with the individual, patient and therapist uncover the unconscious conflicts that prevent the patient from being spontaneous about the way in which they communicate.
- Cognitive-Behavioral therapy, in this case, for individuals, centers on the automatic or distorted thinking patterns that keep the patient from improved functioning and communication. Once the patient is able to

identify their automatic thoughts, they can learn new and more realistic ways of thinking that will improve their mood, self-esteem and how they interact with other people.

As children we are apt to knee jerk our reaction and stop speaking. This can be a learned behavior in the home. Learning constructive ways of dealing with problems was never practiced. What was learned was cover your ears and try to forget what happened by silence – not speaking about it. How much do you still think about it and let it continue to bother you because you don't address the issue? Do you think about it all the time or just periodically? The situation left as a buried unresolved issue is certainly not a healthy situation for anyone mentally or physically.

According to Schwartz, "Research during the past thirty to forty years points to the fact that mind and body are not separate. While the brain resides in, and is protected by the skull, its neurons reach down throughout the entire body. A vast neurological network carries messages to and from every nook, cranny, and corner of the body. What this means is that outside or environmental stimuli which impinge on the external body deeply affect the internal organs, including the brain. He goes on to explain the damage these messages can do. The messages sent from the brain in reaction to the external stimuli then affect those same organs. We now know that stress, anger, aggravation, nutrition, exercise, and other factors profoundly affect the way we feel. Consequently, the immune system is affected, making us more vulnerable to cold viruses. Constant anger and conflict lead to high blood pressure, strokes, heart attacks, and even diabetes. It is now a proven fact that depression resulting from a heart attack, if left untreated, shortens the life span of the recovering patient. In other words, there is more to recovering from a physical illness than restoring good health. Mood, environment, aggravation, and depression, have a negative impact on the ability of a person to return to health. What has this to do with the "culture of not speaking?" Bottling up our emotions and opinions whether you are the silencer or the one silenced profoundly affect one's health.

I wonder if the silent treatment is what led to Frank's illness. I first met Frank several years ago through friends in town. He was seventy years old, retired and battling cancer. At first, he told me he only had a son, but he eventually shared he also had a daughter, Cindy but she didn't exist in his life anymore. He obviously loved and relied on his son but what happened to his daughter Cindy? Frank never spoke about her and if he did it was always how she shut him out of her life and he had no use for her.

I didn't get involved in a lot of the story because he obviously had another point of view. Fortunately, God, or his higher power intervened one Valentine's Eve. "My daughter just called and wants to make me my favorite dinner for Valentine's Day". One way to Frank's heart was through food and Cindy probably knew that. "What should I do?"

This was the daughter he had closed off for many years out of hurt and anger. This was after years of no communication. My suggestion was to have her come over and let her cook. Who would not want mac and cheese made with some creamy cooper cheese found in Pennsylvania! Keep your ears open and listen and your mouth shut was my advice. They got through the first awkward moments and once the cooking began so did the sharing of memories. Frank knew he was dying and so did his daughter. Cindy knew her Dad's medical condition from her brother, Rob whom she also invited to dinner that night. It ended with all three of them spending a happy Valentine's Day and removed the wedge between his son and daughter.

When Frank passed away Cindy and Rob were grateful, they reunited as a family. They also held great sadness about the twenty years they lost because of the harm that was done by the "I can't hear you" attitude. As his daughter, Cindy, sat crying at the funeral, I whispered in her ear. "Your Dad said you were a fantastic cook and made the best mac and cheese in the world." What a smile came on her face.

If we can take a fresh look, be willing to change our outlook, we might be able to change the outcome even after years of not speaking-when the years of silence was not golden. Being able to see the other person's viewpoint and where they are coming from allows us to shift from self to the common good for both. Finally, you begin to see the person who was your enemy and problem in a new light. We can save a lot of pain and time by attempting to hear each other.

Silence isn't golden when:

- We damage each other with silence and avoid difficult conversations
- We believe only our own story
- We stop listening with our heart and don't keep an open mind
- Avoid hearing that inner voice speaking to you.
- We refuse to resolve our old tapes and thoughts
- We let years come between our self and our loved ones

Chapter 6
Running from the Pain

Our culture tends to ignore the pain behind silence. Emotional pain eats at you and occupies a lot of mental time as well as not being good for your overall physical health. The ghosting and silent treatment are only band aids. When we run from anything we may be hiding but we are not escaping ourselves.

Not being able to speak out for what we believe in or feel we want to say is only one reason we run. We run when we are deeply hurt, or someone has spitefully lashed out at us. In silence we are left with all kinds of crazy assumptions as to what might have transpired and some of the time the story, we created in our own minds isn't accurate. Without knowing the true facts by speaking words, there is a tendency to put blame where it doesn't belong. Sometimes we place it on ourselves and that can leave us in a sad lonely place.

There is no such thing as winning a fight, that's for sure. Both parties are hurt in the process, even those that profess to not give a hoot. The phrase, what you resist persists, is true. You will periodically experience that nagging, gnawing sensation that things aren't right.

The stressful pain we feel from the silence causes many changes to whom we are as individuals. We may isolate and withdraw. There is usually sadness if we have cared for the person cutting us off. We can be cut off from family and friends causing separation. Our relationship to the person shunning us will change our behavior. Words matter, no matter who we are. A dark cloud will be with us until we resolve the issue or figure out how we will respond to it and make peace with how we will cope with the silent gap we have created.

The pandemic forced silence on a lot of families. When the pandemic hit, and people became ill, some were in hospitals and others in nursing homes. Mothers and fathers were isolated due to the lockdown in their facilities and were unable to communicate. Family members were unable to travel from state to state due to restrictions. Many residents had problems staying connected with social media. The communication was only as good as their technical knowledge of computers and phones or assistance from their caretakers. If individuals were emotionally close before the pandemic, a strong attempt was made to reach out and stay connected. Sadly a few used silence to bring relief to a troublesome situation.

The pandemic created a convenient excuse for some people to not see each other whether it was due to travel restrictions, quarantines, masks etc. They finally had a legitimate excuse to distance themselves from toxic behaviors, lifestyles, and beliefs.

According to Craig N. Sawchuk, Ph.D., L.P. a clinical psychologist at Mayo Clinic, "More than one-quarter of American adults have cut off contact with a family member, according to a recent large-scale national survey. Family estrangement is a suspension of direct communication between relatives, often triggered by a conflict. In some families, a series of conflicts is followed by periods of avoidance and withdrawal. In others, an incident — potentially even seemingly unrelated to an underlying tension — can be the "last straw."

Not all estrangements are between parents and children — sometimes communication breaks down between siblings or between extended relatives. Estrangement may occur for a variety of reasons. Adult children commonly cut off their parents because of toxic behaviors such as violence, abuse or neglect, or feelings of being rejected. On the flip side, parents often cut ties because they object to a child's dating partner or spouse. Stark differences in beliefs— over subjects such as politics, the pandemic, or vaccinations — can be divisive and may also drive a wedge between family members."

Illness can be a reason we shut down communications and retreat into a corner. The pain of addictions, diabetes, depression and more make us want to create an isolated place where we don't have to interact with others. These types of illnesses can create a deliberate ghosting reaction where you become an obsolete shadow in someone's life. Illness is what tore Jim and Diane apart.

They met as freshmen at Fairleigh Dickinson University in 1966. Jim was twenty-two years-old and Diane was twenty-one. They became friends and hung out together at lunch and breaks between classes. Jim and Diane were both education majors; he was secondary education and she was elementary education. He was from Clifton, NJ a wealthy suburban town and she was from Jersey City, an urban city – truly two different worlds. Diane was comfortable and familiar with Clifton as she spent time with her uncle who lived there.

Jim and Diane did not start dating until after graduation. During Jim's first year teaching, Diane sent him a Christmas card and wrote a note about her difficulties teaching in an urban environment where education was not always a priority with very little parental involvement. She was back home in Jersey City teaching and he was teaching in New Milford, NJ, a suburban town with parents who were very involved in their children's education and success. Jim responded enthusiastically to Diane and she invited him to her house. They spent hours that day sharing great conversation. Diane's mother questioned whether they were more than friends.
Diane said, "No, there is nothing between us."

Jim and Diane's mother hit it off from the very beginning and developed a nice relationship. Her mother said, "This is the guy you should be dating." Shortly thereafter Jim and Diane started going out. They were having a good time – being friends first really helped. The only problem was his mother, Margaret, who did not like her. She had not met Diane, had only seen pictures but called her a bleached blonde, spoiled brat. This did not faze Jim because he had his own issues with his mother. The relationship between Jim and his mother was often filled with quarrels.

When they decided to get married, all hell broke loose with his mother and her sisters. They constantly insulted Diane and her mother. Very little communication happened between the families and Jim stopped communicating with his mother.

Jim and Diane moved to a townhouse community in Secaucus, NJ with a pool, gym, tennis, and racquetball courts. They enjoyed all the amenities and it felt as if they were on a permanent vacation. Both were avid tennis players. Jim and Diane also purchased a townhouse in the Poconos as a weekend and summer residence while they were still working They played golf, raising money for local charities and Jim began to do mission work with the Church, traveling to Cuba, Haiti, and Kenya. This all fell apart when he was diagnosed with diabetes. He was depressed and wasn't willing to follow his diet. As his sugar count rose, he became more depressed. He stopped socializing, did not play much golf, took a leave of absence from teaching, and stayed by himself in the Poconos.

After being married for forty-seven years, Diane was dealing with a diabetic husband who did not take care of himself. He did not want to be told to follow his diet regimen. This loving, caring, generous man turned into a nasty, verbally abusive, and mean person as his diabetes changed his personality. He alienated all his friends in the community. Jim asked for a divorce and within less than two years died. Even though they were divorced it was on paper only. He traveled around and called constantly for help. It was so sad to see his decline and his inability to recognize it in himself. It was always everybody else's fault. Effective communication ceased. There was no way to engage him in conversation, to get him help. Projection upon others, not taking responsibility and blaming others continually blocked any conversation among Jim and his loved ones.

The warm, caring, best friend relationship that started in college that had lasted for over forty –five years died a slow death, partly because Diane never knew who she was coming home to, as Jim became more and more silent when he was not screaming.

Jim did keep in contact after the divorce. When Diane had not heard from him in a couple of months, she got worried. He had a relationship with her cousin in North Carolina, so she placed a phone call to him in the beginning of December to see if he had heard from Jim. This is when Diane found out he was in the hospital and rehab since September. Within a couple of weeks, Jim had deteriorated to the point of being unresponsive and on a respirator. Doctors suggested that he be put into hospice. Within two days after he was taken off medicines he passed away.

"I am glad I never gave up when that little voice inside kept saying, 'hang in there.' Do not abandon him." Jim's girlfriend kept telling the doctors to keep him alive – all the while, taking money from his ATM account every couple of days, even after he died.

In the end Diane was the only one who could put him to rest lovingly, as he had still left her in charge of all his affairs. Even though the communication disappeared between Jim and Diane, she was able to rebuild the bridge back a bit at the end.

Jim and his family never reconciled before his death. A couple of his cousins were in contact but could tell Jim was not the same person they had known.

You would think from this story that Jim didn't give a hoot but that really wasn't the case. It was his diabetes diagnosis and not being willing to follow doctor's orders. We can only be left to assume why the door was shut. Sometimes, if we keep an open mind and wait in love, we will find the real cause of why we should not have abandoned the relationship. It can take years, however. We may be meant to remain in the wings, standing strong and dedicated to the memory of what was for a reason. Only we can decide that.

Put your own pain aside long enough to look at the other person's pain and how they are hurting themselves. Your understanding of their situation and problems may help rectify and repair a bad situation and you may not be left with the experience and pain of a lost relationship.

Silence isn't golden when:
- We run rather than face our situation
- No one looks at the cause of the pain
- We don't look beyond our own pain
- We think winning the fight by silence will make it right
- We take little annoyances for big problems
- Our actions incite an irreparable situation

Chapter 7
Continuing Unhealthy Behaviors

There are two participants in the silent treatment - the silencer and the silenced one. The silencer is the one who makes the first move to silence a relationship –because they feel some hurt, they are angry or depressed. A silencer with passive personality uses it to avoid a difficult issue by not communicating. A stronger personality may use it more for punishment and control.

The one being silenced also doesn't have skills to manage conflicts or be able to communicate in difficult situations. They absorb the hurt instead of choosing not to speak up to the silencer. In time, both people in a relationship can eventually become a silencer. The story of Pamela in Chapter 2 was an example of this. I first silenced her to avoid getting into her unhealthy situation with her husband. She then silenced me in anger for not helping her. We both gave it and got it.

The silent treatment is used by people as a shield from emotional pain and conflicts. We fear being challenged in our beliefs, causing retaliation, or not being liked for speaking our truth. The silencer uses avoidance to gain the upper hand because they don't allow the silenced one to verbally question them.

The silent treatment and ghosting consist of a silencer and the one being silenced that can happen for many reasons. The silencer may stop talking to you or texting very abruptly. They may use this as a way to communicate their emotions in a non-verbal way. Anger and manipulation to avoidance and not being able to express their true thoughts in words, is why the silencer has closed the door on you. *One Day at A Time in Al-Anon* says, "A grim and furious silence can be more crushing and wounding than harsh words."

We usually think of the person that gives the silence as the bad guy. This is not always the case. Time changes us as well as life's circumstances.

This control is powerful and a very unhealthy behavior for both parties in the relationship. Because the silencer is stuffing his emotions down deep, it is likely that over time he will suffer headaches, stomach aches, anxiety, or a host of other physical ailments. The person that has been silenced is locked away and unable to do anything that might fix the situation. It is a punishing behavior that keeps that person bottled up with their feelings. Even though words are not being exchanged between the parties, the relationship still continues as the emotions are left dangling.

Kevin uses the silent treatment with his family to distance himself from anything that causes anxiety or frustration for him. After experiencing 9/11 and seeing the twin towers fall from his office nearby, Kevin explained "I have become a different person." Stress, conflicts, or anything he feels he cannot control bring on severe panic attacks and stomach issues. Simple external stimuli sent Kevin into anger and aggravation. He is constantly worried about his health and physical condition. It is likely Kevin had some underlying depression before 9/11, but that tragedy brought it to the surface.

Kevin never married and his family consists of one living relative, his nephew Bill. Up until 9/11, Kevin and Bill were very close talking weekly and spending holidays together. Kevin believes he has a sense of what is politically correct, and what people should or shouldn't be doing. His strong rigid beliefs have driven his response to people. When Bill began questioning and challenging his uncle's beliefs, he was shut down quickly and eventually permanently. Over the years Kevin turned to prescription drugs and alcohol to further bury his feelings. Sporadic attempts were made at therapy, but nothing consistent enough to work through his anger or depression.

Kevin has become a silencer again and again with work peers and neighbors to maintain emotional distance. His nephew Bill has been left wondering if encouraging Kevin to see a broader and healthier viewpoint was worth it. Bill has lost someone who has meant a lot to him. He was silenced to avoid any type of emotional discussion. Kevin's time is now spent with acquaintances in large groups, so he does not have to reveal anything too personal or respond to prying questions.

In a popular self-help psychology book, *I Don't Want to Talk About It,* psychotherapist Terence Real discusses what he refers to as the secret legacy of male depression. The secret legacy refers to the male value of hiding feelings and appearing strong and masculine. With verbal and emotional pathways of expression closed to them, many men turn to alcohol and/or drug abuse to attempt to defuse their problems. Real's description of male depression fits with Kevin, who describes some of the buried emotions as:

1. Shame
2. Anger
3. Rage
4. Embarrassment
5. Sadness
6. Love and affection for their children

These are only a few examples of hiding or stuffing feelings. Most of us have stories of being the silenced one. At some point, it begins to feel like emotional abuse. When you have been shut down, you have no context or insight into what that person is thinking or feeling. You are left in the dark which only breeds fear and confusion for what is going on in the silencer's heart and mind. It is like dealing with a ghost. All you are left with is wondering and guessing what you did, which can lead to feelings of guilt, anxiety, and shame. It creates anxiety when you can't address the other person's viewpoint or feelings.

Rob became a silencer because of his gambling. In the beginning his friends thought he was going to the casino occasionally for enjoyment. As time went on his friends realized he had a serious addiction issue and at that point he distanced them by ghosting all of them. Rob's shame caused him such embarrassment he couldn't face them anymore. It was easier to run and shut his feelings and friends down with silence. He never spoke to them again. He silenced himself.

Depression over life's circumstances can also turn someone into a silencer. Maggie and Linda knew each other for sixty plus years. They had met freshman year in high school at band. They were both saxophone players and bonded instantly. They went through high school, college, dating and marriages with a lot of memories and history between them. They knew each other's past for years and they could talk and be able to read between the lines without explaining every detail in words. This is very special when you have a long relationship.

As the years went by, both Maggie and Linda had life changing events happen in their lives. Linda had divorced, losing family members, and facing illness in her own life. Maggie's life was much smoother until her later years. She did not have children and life focused on Maggie and her husband's family. Maggie's husband became disabled a few years before they retired, and she started with a chronic cough that led to a severe lung condition. It was a devastating change for both. One thing had always been constant up until this point for both Linda and Maggie. They always helped and supported each other through all of life's ups and downs.

Maggie had come from a family that was very good at ghosting and she was not a stranger to using it herself. As her life was falling apart and she was no longer in control she communicated with a yearly birthday card without a message – just Maggie. Linda occasionally would call to talk. Maggie never divulged much about what was going on in her life and she resisted any talk about coming over to visit them. This went on for ten years. The relationship hung on with a thin icy thread. During their relationship Linda felt less considered at times and shut out by silence. She was sure it had to be her. She would reach out constantly with her tail between her legs inquiring "What went wrong? What did I do? Tell me what I did. Is there anything I can do to make amends?" Linda was groveling to get back into good graces and restore the relationship. You would think she would quit and have more self - esteem, then to crawl, realizing no person should be worth doing this for. A small voice always said, "Try one more time."

After Linda's yearly invitation to Maggie to meet for lunch, she finally agreed to check the calendar. Linda was excited and ecstatic to see her. They caught up on life's challenges, changes, their getting older and left the lunch being glad they had this opportunity to be together.

They both had evolved. In retrospect – the silence wasn't caused by anything that Linda had done. It had to do with Maggie's circumstances involving friends, family members and illness. Maggie isolated not wanting to air her dirty laundry and was not able to reach out emotionally. She always wanted to put the perfect picture of her life out there.

Over lunch Maggie explained her lung condition had worsened. She explained things were confusing and convoluted. After saying good-bye with a hug and the old "I love you" they did keep in touch more consistently by phone. Silence creates unhealthy behaviors and ruins relationships causing isolation and emotional damage. If a little voice is telling you to keep trying and you can't just walk away heed the voice. You may be the person who is supposed to still be in the picture. The phone rang and Maggie said her husband was in the hospital and she needed help.

Maggie was having severe breathing problems, on oxygen and in a wheelchair at this stage of her illness a year later. She asked if I could take her shopping. Another ten months went by. During this time, Maggie's health was deteriorating, and she was bouncing back and forth between the hospital, the rehab, home one night and then calling 911 to send an ambulance for a repeat performance. It was partially her lungs and the rest stress. Maggie emotionally and physically couldn't handle taking care of herself, her sick husband, or her home anymore. During one of their last conversations, she told Linda the nursing home was the vacation she hadn't had for years. Linda and Maggie still did not talk on a regular basis but would text.

One afternoon the nursing home called Linda and said Maggie had asked to see her. Linda was nervous but happy. Maggie asked her to open the bottom drawer of her night table and take out a green gift bag. In it were three pages of handwritten one-line memories from the first time they met until their meeting for their lunch date. Her final wish from Linda was to fill in any memories she missed. They reminisced over fifty years of memories and Linda decided to go back and see her a few days later.

She certainly didn't think that would be the last time she would see her. Maggie gave up. She was not strong enough physically or emotionally to continue with her life. If she hadn't buried everything, mostly thoughts and feelings, and had addressed them earlier might she still be here?

This story was a catalyst for my writing. There was no reward for not speaking from my viewpoint.

Maggie hid the shame of what she thought she, as well as her home looked like. She did not want to admit that life was getting too difficult to handle anymore. What she did get was her own isolation she so desperately wanted. I still sit and ponder why? It was painful to watch the destruction from a distance.

That is why bridging that silence is important – stepping outside your own box to reach out if that little voice keeps nagging you. Will it remedy all our feelings and put us back to where we were? No! We will be creating a new relationship with our present situations and beliefs. If we make the commitment to continue in this new relationship, we will make a choice to put some things that don't work up on the shelf. Instead of silence, love, caring, and honoring of a relationship may well be worth it. Only you can decide.

We can isolate ourselves from dealing with feelings and pain by the silent treatment. If both the silencer and silenced one are complacent, the lingering silence will keep them stuck in their own beliefs and that can be damaging to all. We all have different levels of how we deal with our emotions. If we are the silencer we can't be challenged, criticized, or held accountable for whatever the situation is. We have just disappeared into our own state of beliefs. There was no good ending for this story, and I wonder how wide the gap of silence really was.

Silence isn't golden when:
- Lack of communication interrupts decision making and relationships
- The intention is manipulation
- We insulate ourselves from feelings we can't deal with
- We think there will be a good payoff
- We don't use each relationship as a chance to grow in your own character
- We don't remember what is going on in someone else's life

Chapter 8
Calling it Quits or Forgive?

How do you decide when to close the door on communication and say enough is enough? It depends on each individual and their circumstances. I am not an advocate for slamming the door in silence however physical and emotional well-being may require this.

We are complicated and each of us has our own breaking point. I personally believe there are parts of people we like and dislike at the same time. We are not perfect beings. If we are rigid, we will have an easier time ghosting someone rather than someone who has heard the slogan used in popular recovery programs "take what you like and leave the rest."

When I am in turmoil, I have a hard time thinking my thoughts out and it is better to take a time out before opening my mouth. Emotions of loss, anger, and being left out or being forgotten can be strong triggers for deciding to slam the door. Calling it quits and deciding enough is enough can be a cut off to shut someone out or a remedy to feel better. Both the silencer and the silenced one can choose to permanently cross the gap of silence. It is a two-edged sword. If we are the silencer and cannot find a way to resolve the conflict that keeps us trapped or in a situation that is unresolvable and unhealthy to you a firm calling it quits will bring relief. You will know deep down enough was enough without guilt and hopefully will forgive the person you are in conflict with. This will have brought peace to an intolerable situation. Your heart and body will feel relief – done, over, and a weight will be lifted.

If you are the silenced one calling it quits allows you to walk away and close the situation down on your terms. However, even though you stop speaking with the silencer, you are still in relationship with each other. Eventually you may stop questioning what happened and hopefully find peace.

"There is an enormous physical burden to being hurt and disappointed," says Karen Swartz, M.D., director of the Mood Disorders Adult Consultation Clinic at The Johns Hopkins Hospital. Chronic anger puts you into a fight-or-flight mode, which results in numerous changes in heart rate, blood pressure and immune response. Those changes, then, increase the risk of depression, heart disease and diabetes, among other conditions. Forgiveness, however, calms stress levels, leading to improved health.

Swartz goes on to say, "whether it's a simple spat with your spouse or long-held resentment toward a family member or friend, unresolved conflict can go deeper than you may realize—it may be affecting your physical health. The good news: Studies have found that the act of forgiveness can reap huge rewards for your health, lowering the risk of heart attack; improving cholesterol levels and sleep; and reducing pain, blood pressure, and levels of anxiety, depression and stress. And research points to an increase in the forgiveness-health connection as you age."

There can be situations when you need to close the door for your own sanity and wellbeing and still forgive. You would be doing more harm to yourself and those around you by bringing this person back into your life. I believe in certain conditions and situations that it is in our own best interest to walk the other way when our efforts to open the door of reconciliation would not move the relationship forward. The same situation would go round and round again without any constructive solution. This does not mean we don't forgive the other person; it just means we don't continue with half measure solutions and the same old, same old ways.

Craig N. Sawchuk, a psychiatrist at Mayo Clinic, explains, "there are, however, also situations where a breaking of ties can bring a sense of relief. People sometimes find it necessary and healthy to cut ties with a family member when the relationship involves harmful factors such as abuse — whether physical or psychological — or unwanted manipulation. Still, the emotional toll of taking this step and maintaining distance is often difficult, and you may benefit from the support of a counselor or other mental health professional as you navigate this."

Relationships can go down another path than when they first began. Time can change us and we can grow out of being in sync with each other. Romantic relationships as we know can have this happen and we may say enough is enough and make a quick cut and it's over. Circumstances can create a change in you and your belief system. It can make you feel trapped and wanting to call it quits.

There's one relationship example I want to share that required calling it quits. It was unusual because it combined work and friendship. Terry was caught in a triangle between two business partners who professed to be friends. She worked for Pete and Dick for fifteen years. Over that period, this three-way relationship became like a stick in Terry's eye. Unfortunately, there was a tremendous amount of buried anger and hostility between Pete and Dick. They both needed each other to survive yet they feared and mistrusted each other. Terry was the stability block for many years until she realized how dysfunctional the situation was for her. One day one partner would cry on her shoulder and his story sounded believable, the next day the other would tug at her sympathies with a different story. She felt like a rag doll being torn apart by them. Terry finally decided she had enough and her sanity was more important than her job, and she quit. Enough was enough and to this day, the craziness goes on between them. When you are the one in the middle and things have become intolerable it is doubly hard to have a good outcome.

If she were to walk back into friendship with them nothing would have changed, and Terry would still be in the middle being abused again and taking back all the problems she had struggled so hard to free herself from. She definitely had to practice tough love. Terry has fond memories of the beginning years with Pete and Dick and has to practice forgiveness for all the upset they both had caused in her life. She believes that self - forgiveness was, also, essential for her as a

person and to not feel regret for being the silencer –
and quitter – on the situation.

Terry occasionally rides through the town she
worked in. Pete and Dick lost their shop but continue
a symbiotic relationship. She says a prayer of thanks
for the decision to move onto serenity and a prayer
for a healthier relationship for them. For her it's over
– enough was enough!

Whether you are the cause or not, harboring subtle
resentments causes an underlying tension not good
for your health. Forgiveness to me has nothing to do
with making them or you right or wrong. Forgiveness
to me says you belong on this earth as much as I do,
and I will allow you to be who you are. It doesn't
have to be the fuzzy I love you and making up. It
might be I forgive you, but I am not coming back.

Sometimes we need to pull back and be the silencer
for our own mental health and peace of mind.
Retreating may be the only way to diffuse a battle if
the situation is super charged. What does this
relationship and person mean to you? Looking back at
Pamela's story it is almost impossible to deal
rationally with someone who has severe anger issues
or a mental health problem. Being the silencer may be
the healthiest thing you can do for yourself or the
other person.

The silenced one is the receiver of the silent
treatment and can have their health affected as much
as the one doing the silencing. When you are the
silenced one you are forced to stuff your feelings and
truths about a situation without having a way to speak
your side of the story. Peace may only come when
you detach and let go. We are all capable of being the

silencer and the one being silenced and at times we play both parts.

I personally have been on both sides of calling it quits and I am at peace although reconciliation is always my first choice. How much pain are you willing to endure? Each of us has to make that decision. I have met people who tell me they "don't give a hoot" about a relationship anymore. They can either be the silencer or silenced party. They profess they don't care as if it was over and enough was enough but there still is that tiny question lurking way down inside – why? It really may not be over – maybe we use this attitude as emotional protection from facing the pain and loss we feel from this person.

If we don't give thought to the "why" behind the silence, we aren't really done with it. It's important to truly understand the situation and come to clear terms on why it ended. Ghosting is a substitute for avoidance. Is enough, enough or is there still hope? Each one of us must answer that for ourselves. In the following chapters, you'll discover what you can do to build the bridge back to someone you've silenced or has silenced you.

Silence isn't golden when:
- We use it as a protective shield which separates relationship
- We silence our abusers because we can't reach them by understanding our words
- You can't trust the words you hear

Part 3
Building the Bridge Back

Chapter 9
Questions For a New Start

You've decided that there is someone you've silenced, or has silenced you. What person is important enough in your life that you want to invest the emotional energy necessary to build the bridge back to two-way communication? It takes carefully chosen words and the right attitude to rebuild the bridge. Both the silencer and the silenced one need understanding, truth, and compassion for themselves and each other. The hardest job to opening communication is to look at ourselves honestly and share what we are thinking. It takes a lot of self- reflection.

Conflict and how we address it also determines the outcome. Conflict is a normal occurrence in our daily lives. When we can address the issues without criticism, blame, or feeling less as a person, our relationships become closer and are strengthened by resolving conflict through resolution. We build resistance and learn about ourselves and others when working through conflict.

In the Positive Value of Conflict: The Power of Resolution, Eugene Beresin, professor of psychiatry at Harvard University, explains that there are two types of families that have issues with conflict resolution:

1. Families that never fight where there is no apparent conflict, or hidden conflict.
2. Families in which the conflict is overt, often brutal, and hurtful.

Beresin says, "What is common in these two situations is the *lack of conflict resolution*. In one situation, conflict is denied or hidden. In the other, feelings of rage, harshness, or rigidity do not allow for peace and reconciliation. In both cases, conflict eats away at the needed attachment we have for each other in families, and takes a toll not only on the relationship, but on one's personal sense of security, acceptance, and self-esteem."

Beresin believes that conflict is inherent in human relationships, but resolving the conflict is what makes us closer and enhances the feeling of belonging and attachment to the other person. He notes that resolution does not equal agreement, and in fact, agreeing to disagree is a key ingredient in conflict resolution. Agreeing to disagree, calls upon our ability to have acceptance and tolerance and love for the other person.

Knowledge, truth and listening with our hearts help enlighten us with a deeper meaning of what caused the silent treatment. Our brains are connected to our hearts and souls as well as connected to others. Go beyond the pain and listen to your heart to ask yourself questions that will bring out the truth of the situation.

- Ask questions about what happened and why? Were you and the other person going through difficult times that may have skewed judgment and behaviors?

- Ask questions that would reveal the true essence of the situation? Be willing to look at the parts of the situation you might not know or understand. At times we hardly know ourselves and don't have a crystal ball to see into others' lives.
- Ask questions of yourself first that might bring you to a place of compromise. Are you the one who must always be right and afraid to change your outlook? Both sides matter to resolve a conflict.
- Ask yourself what you are really feeling. Do you feel bad and why? These questions are a fact-finding mission only and you are not locked into anything. Looking at ourselves and the other person are equally important.

Questions contribute to shifting our thinking and possibly coming up with a different conclusion or giving us another possibility of why it happened. Perhaps we will begin to see a little light at the end of the tunnel toward compromise or a solution. If your questions cause you to lose your grip, don't panic. You may be being led to a better way. There is a divine intelligence along with our subconscious that questions as well. Questions help us calmly agree to disagree and can help soften expectations and see the bigger picture of the field we are playing on. Questions widen our view. Challenge your viewpoint and don't be afraid to see other possibilities. Don't be stuck. Relationships of future generations are shaped by what we choose to do. Taking some thought and time to question could be the vision change needed. Question without judgment!

Asking the right questions are the stepping stones to help us repair our path over the bridge and out of silence. I have used these to weed out my own quirky thinking and old tapes.

- Is the problem something I caused, and should I be dealing with it?
- Have I been out of touch with what has happened in the other person's life?
- Is the problem something that wasn't my business?
- Do I trust my own feelings and judgments?
- Do I trust the other person?
- Is this issue caused by my dislike or old tapes or my opinion? Why am I passing judgment? Can we observe rather than instantly judge and look at their essence of who they are?
- Did I examine my motive first, then, look at the other person? Situations and people change.
- Was low self- esteem involved on my part? Do I feel I deserved to get my needs met?
- Was I afraid to change my outlook or want the other person to remain stuck with their viewpoint so my perception of them remained unchanged?
- Can I truly listen to the other person with my heart as well as my ears?
- Can I clearly and truthfully see my part in the disagreement? Could I shift my view slightly and not be narrow minded?
- Can I communicate my feelings and viewpoint calmly, truthfully and without justification or judgment?

- Can I agree to disagree temporarily if we can't resolve the problem and give it space? This is hard when you really think the other person is totally wrong.
- Do I see a temporary time out as a compromise or a partial giving in or honestly want to take an impartial look at my own expectations of the outcome?
- Can I allow others to have their emotions and opinions? These are not mine and I don't have to have my own way and react.
- Can I let the other person know I care and love them and that understanding them is more important to me than being right?
- Can I think before I speak and choose my words and tone of voice wisely? Words do matter as well as tone.
- Am I willing to make my main goal one of restoration and can I extend a little mercy? Will I pray for courage to be truthful in my view of the apple and not be afraid to speak it?

Sarah Schewitz, a clinical psychologist, and founder of Couples Learn, teaches conflict management and communication. She outlines five steps in opening communication:

1. **Stay calm.** Responding in an aggressive way out of frustration or anger makes the situation worse. Staying calm is a way to help you stay in control.
2. **Start a conversation**. Try to find a time when both of you don't have commitments within the next couple of hours. Schewitz notes that it is

important to prepare what you want to say in the conversation so you can keep comments on topic.

3. **Ask what's going on.** No one can read another's mind, so be as encouraging as possible with the other person to have them express their thoughts and feelings as clearly as possible about the situation, and the silence that has come between you.
4. **Invite them to share.** Use open-ended questions to give them different ways to share what has happened in their minds and how they feel.
5. **Explain how you feel about being ignored.** Be clear that the silence between you is making you sad and will continue to damage the relationship if not resolved. Schewitz cautions not to blame the other person for the silence.

Mike and his stepdaughter, Stephanie's relationship is an example of the deep and patient work that is needed to stop the silent treatment and build back the bridge. Their silent treatment started when Mike said casually to Stephanie, "what happened to your face?" She had developed a bad case of acne. Her feelings were hurt, and she wouldn't speak to him for almost two years. Stephanie became the silencer when she and her side of the family stopped speaking to Mike. Relationships have bumps and stumbles and Mike really tripped over his own feet with this remark. He honestly loved her.

When Stephanie became pregnant, she wanted the family reunited and she had to ask herself some questions. Did she honestly like Mike and realize the remark wasn't intentional? Did she trust him enough to know that he did not want to hurt her feelings? How about her own self-esteem and how important is family? She tried texting Mike telling him she had put the bad feelings behind her. She was willing to let Mike know she cared more about him than the remark. Not surprisingly, Mike did not accept her apology at this point. He needed more time to work his thoughts out and accept her apology. He sent her a text saying "No." Mike now became the silencer.

Mike's wife Pam, who is Stephanie's mother, encouraged him to set his intentions and question what he wants, not only for himself but for the family. Does he trust Stephanie's motives to genuinely patch the relationship between them? Mike's feeling became dug in for over a year. During this time, he had that little voice inside that was keeping him uncomfortable. Mike realized it was time to think how he felt about Stephanie and her family and what kind of outcome he wanted. His daughter-in-law had become the silenced one. Pam encouraged Mike to ask himself the important questions to reconcile, especially for his mother who is elderly and is torn between the two of them.

Mike took a leap of faith and reached out to Stephanie and her family explaining that he had not meant to hurt her with his insensitive remark. She was surprised by Mike's phone call. During the past year, Stephanie had taken a broader look and confided to her mother how sad she was to see the family split apart especially since she had the new baby, their grandchild. Stephanie accepted Mike's apology and realized she had been oversensitive and self-conscious about her acne. She had taken a good look at how her own feelings triggered her shutting Mike out. Looking at herself took time, honesty, and self-reflection.

This story of Mike and Stephanie shows, you can't expect the road back and rebuilding the bridge to be easy. There usually is a little mess involved with it. Both used questions as steppingstones and as self-reflection to open the communication and slow down the reactive side and shut down the old tapes.

We are all diverse in our thoughts, backgrounds, and emotions. We are individuals, no two alike and have many different core values and beliefs. I have learned, especially, when I get into these situations where silence could be the outcome to think about these stepping stones. The best outcome will develop if I look at myself first.

Chapter 10
Building the Bridge of Communication Back

A solid relationship resembles a strong bridge; it is a structure carefully constructed through communication and trust. The silent treatment is a type of shock to the structure, battering the relationship bridge until it weakens and crumbles into pieces. I believe we are all capable of having kind, meaningful communication with each other. If you have decided the bridge is worth building back, I want to show you how you can address those unburied emotions that have been silenced with someone important in your life.

There are usually signs that let you know who these people are that you have missing in your life. One sign is that you suddenly find yourself talking about someone who you've silenced or who has silenced you. Another sign is if you are attending a family reunion, marriage or funeral and anticipating silence or hoping if any silence between you and another person will be finally broken. These people keep talking to us subconsciously, and that is an important conversation to listen to. The relationships still exist whether we are speaking or not. Repairing family relationships is the start to bridging the damaging silence.

"Whether you're a parent who hasn't spoken to your adult child in years or a bitter inheritance dispute divided you and your siblings, family estrangement is never a pleasant experience. But it's a fairly common phenomenon," explains Karl Pillemer, Ph.D., a family sociologist, professor of gerontology in medicine at Weill Cornell Medicine, and author of *Fault Lines: Fractured Families and How to Mend Them*. He conducted a nationwide survey on family estrangement. Nearly thirty percent of the 1,340 people who responded said they have experienced such a rift. Ten percent reported being estranged from a parent or child; nine percent from an extended family member, such as a cousin, nephew, or aunt; and eight percent from a sibling. Half of those who had been estranged said the separation had lasted for four years or longer. This translates to 67 million Americans currently estranged from a loved one–and that's likely an underestimate, Pillemer has said, because people are often reluctant to discuss it.

If you've been estranged from a family member for months or years, the mere thought of resuming contact might stir up a lot of uncomfortable emotions. But maintaining relationships with family is an integral step toward preserving your physical and emotional health. <u>Being lonely or disconnected from others</u> is associated with many health risks, including early mortality.

When I have personally been engaged in the silent treatment, I try to implement the following actions which I hope will work for you, too:

- **Quieting yourself and the chatter that is going on in your head**
  When someone cuts you off silencing yourself is a good place to start? My first reactions were

to call the person, leave all kinds of messages and beg to find out why they weren't speaking to me anymore. The assumption was it was my fault, and I must be the one to find out the cause and fix it. Sometimes situations got too complicated with family and friends and when the issues were so convoluted and complex, the easiest for some of them was to just shut you down and not deal with it. Sometimes we are caught between two poles.

- **Breathe; relax a little then try to put the emotions on the side for a little bit**.
  Think facts and what you see as the truth. Perhaps reflect on how much this person and relationship means to both of you. How bonded were you? If you don't know the facts and reasoning for the silent treatment you are apt to make incorrect judgments and come to wrong conclusions. Try to ask yourself the question what do you think went wrong? A little time out on your part maybe what saves you from overreacting and retaliating.

- **Fear and worry should not stand in your way of reaching out**
  When you are ready to bridge the silence, look at yourself and your position first. If you are the one that has been silenced, you will probably be the one to reach out and ask why? There is no guarantee that you will immediately find out what happened but a phone call, letter, even a text to try to open the communication again is worth a try. A little maturity can help here. Hopefully, the person who silenced or ghosted

you won't hide out for too long and you can begin to ask, "Hey what happened?" The amount of love and empathy you have for each other as well as not making judgments from old tapes will help.

- **Get clear on what we perceive or believe about the other person**
  Look at ourselves and our position first. We know our side at this point but not theirs until we can open a dialogue with the other person. There is no timeline on how to precede only a gut feeling that this bond you have should not end this way. I would suggest not taking anything for granted relating to what happened unless you know why you were the one that provoked the other person or did something to them that caused anger or hurt. As you have seen in some of the stories mentioned in this book there are all kinds of reasons. Some are afraid of the conversation; some just overreact and then are not even sure why they silenced the other person but don't know how to come back to the relationship. Don't believe everything you think, hear, or feel until you have knowledge of what might have happened. Don't let the irrational fears take hold. It is better to wait a little with our words until our thoughts are clear, but we don't have to wait until we are totally in the mood either.

- **If you are the one giving the silence, try to figure out what happened.**
  You may absolutely know why you crossed over the bridge into silence, or perhaps did you

overreact and knee jerk? If you are the one that has been silenced, you may have no clue and feel confused, hurt and maybe angry.

Trust your gut, your higher power and the love or bond you have with this person to guide you. A little time out to regroup may be better than a destructive word at this point that is filled with bitterness and anger. Many things from timing to patience and our commitment to this relationship are at stake.

- **A wide-angle lens view at this stage of the game might save regrets later.**
  Even if your life is filled with other healthy, happy relationships, any estrangement has the power to create feelings of sadness, loss, anger, betrayal, confusion, helplessness, or anxiety, says Tina Gilbertson, L.P.C., author of *Reconnecting with Your Estranged Adult Child: Practical Tips and Tools to Heal Your Relationship* and host of a weekly podcast for estranged parents called The Reconnection Podcast.

  If you're ready to reconnect, here are five steps Gilbertson recommends for rekindling an estranged relationship:

Step #1: Put Yourself in the Other Person's Shoes

Take the time to imagine how a person might have been hurt by whatever perceived wrongdoing occurred in the relationship. Gilbertson says. "If you can't put yourself in the other person's shoes, you won't have any success in reconciling with someone who wants distance."

Step #2: Use Therapy to Grow as a Person Before Reaching Out

Gilbertson calls this "a prerequisite for reconnecting." You don't want to be the same person you were when you became estranged. Look for a therapist with experience in working with individuals experiencing family conflict, who can offer support and help you cultivate insight into your situation. Specifically, you want someone who can offer empathy and an open ear. This type of support is more helpful in estrangement, according to a 2019 study published in the journal *Family Relations*.

Step #3: Reach Out and Take Responsibility

"A heartfelt apology is often the only way to get through to someone who has checked out of a family relationship," Gilbertson says. You want to take responsibility for your part in the falling out. Blame is not always even, and not completely one-sided. Compromise takes two. You can start with something like, I'm sorry I haven't called you in a while. I've done a lot of thinking and I'm ready to take responsibility for my part. The goal is to "Come from a place of generosity rather than blame," Gilbertson says. "If you want reconnection, you need to take on the work of making it happen and focus on connecting with them". If you want to reconcile you have to be the person willing to reach out and perhaps the other person will try also.

Step #4: Hold the First Meeting in a Neutral, Public Setting

Meeting in a public place can help keep the conversation productive and minimize drama. It's easier for tempers to flare in your home rather than in a restaurant or public place. Another option is to meet in a therapist office.

Step #5: Know That Things May Not Work Out (But There's Still Some Success in Having Tried)

Hopefully, reconciliation will work. If not, you put your best effort out there. Be at peace knowing that you tried. This process can be very healing. We can only control ourselves in what we say and do. Even if the person says, it's too late you tried and that can be very cathartic.

Each party holds a piece of the puzzle and if you are committed to repairing this relationship some honest thinking will help. Put the judgments, old tapes, fragile egos on the back burner if possible until you can ask yourself some questions. If you do nothing you will never know. Remember, we can always use our voice, words matter. People matter and the worst that can happen is the silent treatment continues.

I was taking a flight home to PA from Michigan. The plane was flying at a low altitude and as I looked out the window, I saw the lights on the Delaware

River Toll Bridge. Prior to looking out the window I had spent the whole ride fretting and thinking about the situations and problems that were awaiting me. Then I looked out the window at the view. From that window the view was peaceful, beautiful, and serene and all my anxiety vanished. I was seeing the bigger picture through a wider lens and not every little, microscopic detail of my own perspective. Thoughts vanished for a moment giving me a time out to relax and regroup my thoughts on what I was returning home to.

Practicing the wide-angle lens approach allows me to see the broader picture and maybe a few extra viewpoints I might not have thought of. It also takes the focus off every little nitpicky imperfection I might see. The larger view helps to relinquish my anger and lowers the temperature of my upset. Silence creates a big divide and doesn't allow any room to create a clean space for a new beginning.

Relaxing and looking at the bigger reason we were silenced or why we silenced someone might be a good place to start. Finding and examining the truth and sorting out emotions first are better than the reacting to the microscopic details at first. We can have bad days, be tired, not feel good and then decide to knee jerk and cut the other person off for any number of reasons. Honest communication and confrontation can be painful especially if we weren't taught how to express our needs and use silence instead.

I am blessed to not resort to silence when I can't communicate my thoughts properly. I will stammer over my words and perhaps nothing seems to come out correctly as I attempt to convey my message. Talking is the only way I know how to let you know who I am and what I am thinking. I may take a brief time out to think and reflect on the bottom line of what happened but silence for me isn't an option.

If we can let go of old thoughts and tapes taking a fresh wide angle look at the issue, we will find it easier to investigate and discern the facts and truth and be able to make better decisions. Do not be afraid to reach out, be a little humble and vulnerable. Nothing will hurt or harm a relationship as much as the broken bridge of silence.

Here are the elements necessary to help build the bridge back:
- Trust
- Communicating
- Compromise
- Respect
- Patience
- Humility
- Forgiveness
- Understanding
- Truth
- Re-evaluation
- Kindness
- Love
- Seek facts
- Look with wide angle lens
- Listening
- Tolerance

Chapter 11
Regaining Trust

Have you figured out where to begin and rebuild the trust that was lost and taken a time out to think, question and reflect upon the situation? If you have decided to give a shot at bridging the silence trusting yourself and the other person, then begin. You must also feel safe with that other person. It saddened me to hear the regret of those I interviewed, and my own experiences with lost time in relationships due to silence and mistrust. We usually put trust in God, and we must trust ourselves. We must trust that we may make correct assumptions and discern the truth.

You won't know if you don't try. I encourage you to have a positive open mindset so there will be an opening to begin a conversation and reconnect. This can be a character-building moment for the one silenced as well as the silencer. Take the opportunity to grow and rebuild. Perhaps the relationship won't be the same as before, but it has an opportunity for truth and clarity. Somebody has made the first move. The words just need to be sincere, kind, respectful and simple. Some love and empathy could go a long way here. Break down a few walls by relinquishing your views and judgments to start. Listen with open ears and heart. Be prepared, strengthening the bridge to communication will take time and a little work.

Our personal tolerance level to feelings and emotions differs. Don't compare yourself to another. Decide what you want to accomplish, how you want to be in this situation and step forth and be that person. Small steps –little by little.

I met a woman, Marlene, who had just become a believer in Jesus. Growing up her family had not been believers and she grew up without religion. Whether you believe in nature or some form of higher power, you must have trust in it. As an adult Marlene decided to put her trust in Jesus and traveled back home to share this with her mother. Her mother, Joan had bad experiences with religious people and distrusted them. To Marlene's amazement and anguish her mother silenced her for over a year out of distrust and would not speak to her. Marlene had put her trust in God and trusted herself and was confident she made the correct decision. If she hadn't had trust in herself, she might have reverted to being a non-believer. She also trusted that the right outcome would come for Joan.

She attempted periodically to call or text her mother while accepting she would not get an answer. Marlene kept leaving messages. She loved her mother and shared how Jesus loved her and how blessed she was in her new belief. To her surprise her mother began to question and investigate, what her daughter was sharing with her and longed to bridge their broken relationship. A year later, Marlene made a call to her mother, and she answered. She told Marlene she loved her and wanted to know more about her life and her religion. Fortunately, Marlene never gave up and kept sharing small steps to repair their relationship. The broken bridge of communication was not only repaired but strengthened. Both had practiced trust in themselves, each other, and God.

We are often frustrated if there isn't an overnight fix. Again, patience and time can be what will begin to soften years of buried anger, hurts and emotions. We don't know if what we heard, or thought is influencing this if we are honest with ourselves. We are complicated individuals including those that think they have a black or white mentality. The better we understand ourselves the better the outcome. Don't be afraid to change your attitude if needed. A little softening will not weaken your position. You might be heard better. Listen to what that little voice inside you is trying to communicate. It might make a big difference in your relationship.

Don't be afraid to care about the person you silenced or has silenced you. Empathy for yourself as well as the other will open the door to how you will ask the questions and answer them, how vulnerable you will be, how stuck in your own judgments you will be and how forgiving.

Believe you can say your truth, no matter what, if you say it with clarity, respect and a genuine wanting to have the other person understand you. Share who you are, the good and the not so good. Unless we do, we will not be able to keep the conversation and communication going to rebuild the brokenness silence causes. "It is the disease of not listening….that I am troubled with," said William Shakespeare. To repair lost communication, you must listen. To listen not only with your ears but your heart is important to rebuilding trust.

Darlene Lancer, a licensed marriage and family therapist, and author of numerous books and articles on codependency, trauma, and shame says that "once trust has been broken, an apology may not be sufficient to rectify damage to the relationship. Explanations and excuses can make matters worse. She offers these seven steps on how to rebuild trust:

1. Listen to the other person's anger and hurt feelings.
2. Empathize with them.
3. Ask what is needed to prevent a recurrence.
4. Be conscientious to do all the things listed that show trustworthiness.
5. Take full responsibility for your actions. Don't sidestep the issue or try to shift blame to the other person.
6. Make a heartfelt apology expressing your regret.
7. Continue to have open and honest communication.

Building back trust after you have experienced the silent treatment is not easy but essential to rebuilding the bridge that connects you. Both the silencer and the one silenced must rebuild belief in each other and the faith they once had in the relationship before it was shattered. I believe you must not only have trust in each other but trust in yourself first to discern what happened and why. As you can see in the article by Darlene Lancer trust issues begin when we are young and can carry over into all our adult relationships. Rebuilding that trust includes revisiting your old tapes and feelings, empathy, and being your word in relationships. Lack of trust can be a deal breaker when it comes to the silent treatment, and you must be willing to mend it before you can repair the bridge.

Patience with yourself and the other party is a plus. Try to have patience to sit back and take a moment to reflect and think about why the reason for the silence. Take some time to ask questions before being reactive. Pondering a situation instead of acting on impulse and lack of control requires strength to look inward. Patience isn't a virtue of mine, and it takes a lot of restraint for me to practice this, however, I make better decisions for myself and others when I slow down and don't rush things.

Empathy for yourself and the other person is also necessary to determine what went wrong with the communication. Understanding where you are in this disagreement is important. Trying to put yourself in the other person's shoes may help you see across the bridge as to why you silenced or were silenced by the other person. If we don't attempt to see the other side, we might miss out on possibly realizing the options or circumstances from which they had to choose. Perhaps you will take a cooler approach if you attempt to be the bridge and try to communicate with them. A gentle approach with understanding can be strong and a gentle response powerful. Silence can speak louder and harsher than any words.

Time is important. We each have a certain amount of time allotted to us. It is better to not waste a moment of it. The young have a harder time understanding this. Time doesn't wait for anyone, and I encourage everyone to give some thought to this. Don't be complacent and feel time doesn't matter. Looking back at all my stories will show you, you don't have forever to make amends or rekindle that lost relationship over words spoken. It might take quite a bit of time and effort to cross this bridge of silence, or if you are lucky, your attempt to reach out might be met with open arms.

Not everyone has the strength or courage to be the first. What gives me courage in these circumstances is the discomfort I feel if I don't at least to try. I heard a song once that had the lyrics that went something like this "you can't dance with the devil on your back." For me to shake this feeling I at least try. If the person, family member etc. and I have had a very deep bond and relationship I have learned to take a little time and keep the door open for them. That doesn't mean I stay stuck for years but sometimes at least keeping the door unlocked, if not open may be part of the plan for you with them. Perhaps realizing you both may have to grow and mature into a new way of being and thinking before you can view things differently in a situation, is what time can buy you.

Remember words can start a fire. Trust, patience, empathy, and time may give you both a chance to be heard and not waste precious time you might regret. Repair the brokenness, if possible, be the bridge. You and your loved one are worth it.

This piece from author Frank Sonnenberg sums up what I believe, and I hope it will help each of us to have an easier time with all our relationships. He has many stepping stones to help us build back the broken bridge of silence such as promoting a win-win, encouraging we, rather than us vs. them, prove your intentions through actions rather than words and when in doubt, do what's right. Remember trust takes a long time to develop but it can be lost in seconds.

My hope is that you will rebuild back the bridge to communication with the relationships that matter the most in your life.

Endnotes

Chapter 1

How the Silent Treatment Hurts Children.
https://www.dovechristiancounseling.com/the silent
treatment –a form of abuse

Kipling Williams,
https://www.purdue.edu/newsroom/experts/ostracism,
-silent-treatment,-rejection-and-social-
psychology.html

Chapter 5

Stuffing It: The Culture of Not Speaking, Allan
Schwartz, LCSW, Ph.D.,
www.mentalhelp.net/blogs/stuffing-it-the-culture-of-
not-speaking-v2

Chapter 6

*Mayo Clinic explores: The mental health toll of
family estrangement,* Craig N. Sawchuk, Ph.D., L.P.,
November 8, 2021,
mcpress.mayoclinic.org/emotional-health/mayo-
clinic-explores-the-mental-health-toll-of-family-
estrangement

Chapter 7

Terrence Real, *I Don't Want to Talk About It*, Scribner & Sons 1997

Chapter 8

Karen Swartz, M.D., director of the Mood Disorders Adult Consultation Clinic at The Johns Hopkins Clinic
https://www.hopkinsmedicine.org/health/wellness-and-prevention

Mayo Clinic explores: The mental health toll of family estrangement, Craig N. Sawchuk, Ph.D., L.P., November 8, 2021,
mcpress.mayoclinic.org/emotional-health/mayo-clinic-explores-the-mental-health-toll-of-family-estrangement

Chapter 9

Eugene Beresin, The Positive Value of Conflict: The Power of Resolution
www.claycenter.org
https://www.psychologytoday.com/us/contributors/eugene-beresin-md-ma?page=2

Sarah Schewitz, PsyD. Licensed Clinical Psychologist,
https://anchor.fm/daveglaser/episodes/What-is-Safe-Conflict-Resolution-with-Dr--Sarah-Schewitz--type-8-e8fr20

Sarah Schewitz, founder of Couples Learn
https://coupleslearn.com

Allan Schwartz
https://www.allanschwartztherapy.net

Chapter 10

Karl Pillemer, Ph.D.Fault Lines:Fractured Families
and How to Mend Them

Tina Gilbertson, L.P. Reconnecting with your
Estranged Adult Child: Practical Tips and Tools to
Heal your Relationship

Chapter 11
Darlene Lancer, "How to Rebuild Trust in 7 Steps,"
Psychology Today, September 2, 2021
https://www.psychologytoday.com/us/blog/toxic-
relationships/202109/how-rebuild-trust-in-7-steps

About the Author

Carol Stockdale was born in Queens, NY but moved to Chicago at the age of two and spent her happiest years in the Midwest and on Lake Michigan. She now resides in the Pocono Mountains of Pennsylvania with her dog, a rescued Chihuahua, named Rosie and plays tenor sax in a Big Band. Spare time is used to volunteer at her church and the local animal shelter. She totally enjoys spending time with her two children and five grandchildren who always share enthusiasm, wisdom and lots of laughter.

As a young woman, Carol always inspired openness and trust from those who needed to talk about their situations and feelings. Her daily readings of Adult

Children of Alcoholics enabled her to recognize how important honest, clear communication is.

Carol is a first time author sharing her personal family struggles with the silent treatment as well as stories of personal interviews. Losing a relationship you care about leaves emotional as well as physical scars if not remedied. Included in this book is why the silent treatment damages relationships and how to repair the bridge back to healthy communication.

www.ingramcontent.com/pod-product-compliance
Lightning Source LLC
Chambersburg PA
CBHW020600160726
47991CB00002B/801